MERCHANT FLEETS

BLUE STAR LINE

DUNCAN HAWS

Illustrations by Duncan Haws

Scale 1 : 1200

Contents

First published in 1988.

British Library Cataloguing Publication Data

Haws, Duncan
Merchant Fleets 14
Blue Star Line
1. Merchant Marine-History
1. Title

ISBN 0 946378 10 X

The Starling Press Ltd., Risca, Newport, Gwent. NP1 6YB
TCL Publications, Travel Creatours Ltd., 1 Meadowbank Road, Hereford. HR1 2ST.

Introduction

Firstly a word of explanation. Three years ago this volume arrived coincidentally at the selfsame printers a few weeks ahead of the World Ship Society's work on the Blue Star Line. The aim of that noble Society is the same as my own—to foster interest in all things Maritime. Rather than risk damaging their market by a competing book I withdrew. Nevertheless having announced the volume the continuing world-wide requests indicate that there is a demand for a new Blue Star book. Thus the work has been brought up to date (March 1988) ready for publication.

It is now almost eighty years since the Vestey family entered the business of shipowning and during these years the name Blue Star has received justified world-wide acclaim. Their magnificent funnel livery has caused many to hail it as the most beautiful afloat (just as British Caledonian's colours rank similarly in the air). Nor is it apocryphal that in these days of the 'box-boat' Blue Star vessels are designed with funnels capable of displaying to full advantage those majestic colours. Across their global spread of routes there can be no port where the merest onlooker cannot immediately identify Blue Star.

But a funnel is not enough—since the middle twenties the company has established itself in the very forefront of advanced ship design. Good ships look good and this is never truer than with Blue Star.

Technological change has wrought its havoc. The move to containerisation is reflected everywhere. In the case of Blue Star where once a fleet of forty ships traversed the oceans this still thrusting and thriving concern now owns less than a quarter of this total. But, in tribute, the modern fleet flourishes, chartered ships with Blue Star names and livery serve them well and their ship-husbandry can be seen in their Blue Star Ship Management, Merlion, Lion Shipping and Vancouver activities. Finally may I thank those in Blue Star who have so readily made their records available to me. Modestly they request anonimity. As one so aptly put it 'The Company speaks for itself.'

Duncan Haws
April 1988

Explanatory Notes

1 Company histories are arranged chronologically.

2 The ships owned are listed virtually chronologically except that sister ships are grouped together even when the period of their building covers more than one year.

3 Tonnage: the method of calculating tonnage has changed several times since 1830 and very few ships kept their initial tonnage. The gross and net tonnages shown are generally those recorded when the ship first entered service.

4 Dimensions: unless recorded as 'overall' the figures given are the registered dimensions between perpendiculars.

5 The speed given is service speed. This could vary according to route and ports of call.

6 Abbreviations:

Apr	*April*
Aug	*August*
BHP	*Brake horse power*
Blr	*boiler*
B	*Built*
B	*Bridgedeck*
b	*bale*
BSSM	*Blue Star Ship Management*
C	*Cargo*
cabin	*Cabin class*
comp	*compound*
cu	*Cubic*
Cyl(s)	*Cylinder(s)*
D	*Dimensions*
dbl	*Double*
Dec	*December*
Dft	*Draught/draft*
disp	*Displacement*
dk	*deck*
dwt	*Dead weight*
E	*East*
E	*Engine*
exp	*expansion*
F	*Forecastle*
Feb	*February*
ft	*Feet*
fwd	*Forward*
g	*Gross/grain*
GPM	*Goal post masts*
GRT	*Gross registered tonnage*
H	*Hull*
HP	*Horse power/High pressure*
IHP	*Indicated horse power*
in	*Inch(es)*
ins	*Insulated*
Jan	*January*
kts	*Knots*
lb	*Pound(s)*
LP	*Low Pressure*
m	*Metre*
Mar	*March*
MP	*Medium pressure*
n	*Net*
N	*North*
NHP	*Nominal horse power*
Nov	*November*
oa	*Overall*
obb	*over bulbous bow*

Oct	*October*
Pad	*Paddle*
P	*Passengers*
P	*Poop*
Prom	*Promenade*
Psi	*lbs per square inch*
Q	*Quarterdeck*
quad	*Quadruple/four*
refrig	*Refrigerated*
reg	*Registered*
RHP	*Registered horse power*
rpm	*Revolutions per minute*
S	*South*
S.SA	*Stroke, Sgl acting*
S.DA	*Stroke, Dbl acting*
scr	*Screw*
Sept	*September*
sgl	*Single*
SHP	*Shaft horse power*
Stm	*Steam*
Stm P	*Steam pressure*
SV	*Sailing vessel*
T	*Tons*
TEU	*Twenty foot equivalent units*
tpl	*Triple/three*
tst	*tourist*
Turb	*Turbine*
tw	*Twin/two*
W	*West*

BLUE STAR LINE

CHRONOLOGICAL HISTORY

The Industrial Revolution, coupled with population growth, marked the translation of the European states from an Agrarian society into the modern understanding of a supply and demand economy. Barter had long since been overtaken (but not obliterated) by the use of money and wages had become the norm in towns or cities where the service components of society (shopkeepers, lawyers etc.) produced no tangible saleable products. But with the absence of mass-production the economy operated on a low-key basis with little or no need for any marketing skills.

Suddenly, at the end of an era of exploration and colonisation, coal and steam heralded a growth in both product and demand which by the mid-nineteenth century had created vast new markets and the meagre beginnings of the affluent society of today. Among the more significant changes was export and import market growth. The people who had colonised the world beyond the oceans wanted the merchandise of the European industrial revolution; in return they offered the produce of their lands: meat, dairy produce, wool, spices, tea, rice, valuable minerals and precious stone. It was meat and dairy produce that was most needed to feed Europe's burgeoning populations. Great Britain, the motherland to so much of the further transoceanic world, was by now unable to produce sufficient food to satisfy demand. The dictat 'export or starve' was but vaguely understood nevertheless Britain's Industrial Revolution produced the goods that bought the food to Britain's shops. The refrigeration of meat to keep it from rotting had arrived by 1860 but had not been extended to seagoing ships.

1877 It was the French steamer *Paraguay* which carried the first cargo of frozen carcases across the Atlantic from Buenos Aires to Rouen.

1879 The first attempt from Australia, by John Harrison, failed when the ammonia refrigerant leaked.

But in the same year Anchor Line's *Circassia* had a successful working plant installed.

It was now that the Vestey Bros partnership was formed in Liverpool by William and Edmund Vestey. They entered the meat trade with their own cold store and supplied their own retail shops.

The men were not new to the retail trade; both had entered the storekeeping business of their father, Edmund Vestey Senior, on their respective twelfth birthdays. At this stage of their careers, however, they did no more than act as wholesale purchasers from existing frozen meat importers. Nevertheless the business of the young men prospered and their chain of shops grew steadily. In parallel the demand for the fresh meat, made available by freezing, expanded dramatically.

1897 Aug: The Vestey's formed the Union Cold Storage and Ice Company in Liverpool for the purpose of storage and distribution. They became purveyors to all and sundry with such satisfactory results that this activity soon became the mainspring of their enterprise. Their influence extended overseas and grew over the coming years.

1903 The company was re-styled as the Union Cold Storage Co Ltd and continued to develop.

Their main source of meat was from the pampas of the Argentine and their principal supplier was the Royal Mail Steam Packet Co. This company was at this time in poor shape and operated an aging fleet. When Owen Phillips (later Lord Kylsant) took over he immediately commenced a programme of revitalisation and called up the long dormant 40% of unpaid stock. Nevertheless he was not able to agree to the Vestey demand for lower prices nor was he able to match some of the competitive rates being charged by other shippers. The effect was to lower the Union Cold Storage profits despite business growth. It was a situation that the Vestey brothers had to resolve.

1904 Union Cold Storage commenced to charter refrigerated ships on single voyage bases to meet peak demand. In parallel they established their own purchasing organisation in Buenos Aires, founding it upon the contacts made before the turn of the century.

1909 Two refrigerated ships were purchased by Vestey Brothers from Shaw, Savill and Albion: *Pakeha*, which was renamed *Lizanka*, and *Rangatira*. After only one voyage to South America both were chartered to the Russian Government for use out of Vladivostok as mother ships to the Siberian salmon fishing industry. The name *Lizanka* fitted well into Russian but *Rangatira* was renamed *Count Muravieff* for the duration of the charter; at the end of which they reverted to Vestey ownership as *Brodmore*. Strangely *Milonstar*, as *Dnepr*, was to follow an almost parallel career 50 years later.

1910 Vestey Bros acquired Thos. B. Royden's *Indraghiri* which became *Brodstone* (I) and initiated the prefix *Brod* which was to last until the reorganisation at the end of the First World War. Vestey's trade was initially to both South America and China but the later failed to live up to expectations and although attempts were made from time to time to develop the frozen pork trade it failed to come up to expectations.

1911 July 28: Blue Star Line Ltd was formed with Union Cold Storage as the parent holding company. The Blue Star head office was in London at Holland House, Bury Street. The initial capital was set at £100,000.

When, some years later, the company moved to 34 Leadenhall Street the date over the entrance was (and still is) 1909 and not 1911 in recognition of Vestey Bros' three ships.

1912 Jan: Blue Star Line commenced operation with ships having the prefix *Brod* and each owned by a single ship company of the same name. The fleet was *Brodstone* (I), *Broderick* (ex *Lizanka*), *Brodmore*, *Brodland* and *Brodvale*. All five were second hand tonnage and this was a policy which lasted until *Montilla* in 1917.

Nov: *Brodvale* took coal from Barry Docks to Shanghai and loaded frozen pork as the inward freight. After this voyage *Brodvale* was transferred to the River Plate service.

1913 Jan: *Brodland* became the company's first marine casualty when she was wrecked on Aberavon Beach, South Wales.

During this year William Vestey was made a baronet to become Sir William Vestey, Bart.

1914 Aug 4: The First World War commenced while Blue Star was still in its early formative years. Only five vessels were owned at the outbreak; these were *Broderick*, *Brodmore*, *Brodstone*, *Brodvale* and *Brodmount*. A sixth ship was acquired when the *Yula*, building for Stott (Baltic) Steamers Ltd, was bought on the stocks to become *Brodhurst* at her launching and the first newly built ship to enter the company's service even though she was not ordered by Blue Star.

1915 Blue Star were unable to meet all the demands for food brought about by the inevitably reduced number of ships remaining in commercial service. Meat from neutral Argentine was plentiful and to carry the cargoes additional vessels were acquired. Three second-hand ships came from the Scottish Shire Line; *Morayshire* joined the fleet as *Brodliffe* and her sisters *Banffshire* and *Nairnshire* became *Brodness* (8) and *Brodholme* (10) respectively. From Federal S.N. Co came *Surrey*, which had been abandoned to the Government charterers at London with mine damage. She became *Brodfield* (II) and their *Kent* emerged as *Brodlea* (12). Whilst *Rakaia*, virtually a sister to *Whakanui (Brodmount* (6)) was purchased from the New Zealand Shipping Co to become *Broadmead* (13). These six ships doubled the size of the fleet to eleven. At this time a considerable proportion of the Blue Star frozen meat came from Madagascar. Vestey's had always set much store by their own quality control methods and this normally meant setting up their own purchasing and freezing organisations. Now, at Majunga, they set up a French subsidiary Compagnie Générale Frigorifique. Two coasting vessels were built in Scotland, *General Pau* and *General Foch* (159/160) together with two equal sized lighters for them to tow, *General Jarvoni* and *General Marcus*. Their task was to collect live, and tinned, meat from the coastal out stations and transport it to Majunga for handling. This venture was really only a temporary expedient but it lasted until the war was over.

1916 The British Government had met the need for fresh produce and frozen meat by allowing most of the Shaw, Savill & Albion, Federal, P & O and New Zealand Shipping refrigerated ships to continue in commercial, but controlled, service. They had also sanctioned the purchase (and renaming in time of war) by Blue Star of the six ships in 1915. Now three berths were allocated for the building of new refrigerated non-standard ships which were to become the first newbuildings for Blue Star. But perhaps it should be mentioned that *General Pau* was initially owned by Blue Star while awaiting the formation of Cie Générale Frigorifique.

Nov 13: *Brodfield* (11) was wrecked on the Scillies at Church Point.

1917 *Montilla* (14) and *Rubiera* (15) were delivered at a cost of £100,000 each.

Mar 31: *Brodness* (8) ex *Banffshire* was caught and sunk by a submarine off the Italian coast when sailing from Genoa to Alexandria in ballast.

Aug 15: *Brodstone* (4) was lost enroute Cardiff-Zarate.

Dec 27: *Brodmore* (2) was torpedoed north west of Marsa Susa.

1918 *Camana* (16) was the third of the war time trio to be completed.

Apr 29: *Broderick* (1), the initial ship of the fleet, was torpedoed off Hastings outward bound with a general cargo thus becoming the company's last casualty of the war.

Nov 11: The signing of the Armistice denoted the ending of hostilities during which Blue Star had lost five ships and accepted into service three newbuildings to give a fleet of nine. Of this number only four were modern; the remainder were all around twenty years old. A replacement programme was at once put into operation. The first vessel to be acquired was the Standard 'G' type refrigerated ship *War Charon* which had been launched on November 2nd. The name given to her was *Royalstar*, thereby introducing the nomenclature which, with one modification, has remained one the hallmarks of the company ever since.

1919 Jan 24: *Royalstar* (17) ran her trials and was accepted into service. She was followed, in June, by a sister Ship *Albionstar* (18).

Oct: *Normanstar* (24) was completed. These ships gave redoubtable service and the firm was later to purchase three more of these old warhorses.

Dec: *Empirestar* (22) was delivered to complete the quartet of deliveries. However, during the year, a fifth ship, the 26 year old *Magicstar* (23) was bought second hand from Houlders. Despite her age she was good enough to last another eleven years.

1920 March 31: Blue Star Line (1920) Ltd was formed to manage or to bare-boat charter the existing fleet of sixteen vessels—all of which were refrigerated. However for fiscal reasons, mainly tax losses and capital allowances (which the new company could not yet accrue) the parent concern, Union Cold Storage Co Ltd, became in April and May the registered owners of many of the ships. The funnel of the new concern was enhanced by the addition of the now famous black and white bands at the bottom of the black top thereby producing what very many shiplovers hold to be the finest looking stack afloat. At this time the darker pillar-box red was lifted to the bright orange red of today.

The new company was not at this stage a member of the South American Freight Conference; indeed their entry was blocked by some of the existing participants. Blue Star controlled its own meat supplies out of the Argentine and always carried full inbound cargoes however outward cargoes were much more difficult to come by and their ships all too often had to voyage out in ballast. This uncomfortable state of affairs was to last for a number of years to come.

Viking Star (25) was the only new ship during this year. All the 'Brods' were given '*star*' names.

1921 Edmund Vestey, like his brother, was honoured with a baronetcy. *Doricstar* (26) introduced into Blue Star the basic design of big ship which was to become so much a part of the future. Built with massive refrigerated capacity, fast, and with a simplistic uncluttered profile she was nevertheless a strikingly handsome vessel. Oddly, considering the 1920 restructuring she was registered as being owned by Eastman's Ltd, the butchers' shop chain within the group. She was to be their only ship.

1922 Sir William Vestey was created Lord Kingswood.

Oct: Commercial Properties Ltd was formed to take over all the retail shops, including Eastman's, together with all the non-maritime interests. Union Cold Storage took over all the ships with Blue Star Line (1920) Ltd as managers and operators.

1924 *Trojanstar* (29) joined the fleet; formerly *La Perouse*, she was one of six virtual sister ships built during 1915-1917 of which three, *Cumberland*, *Westmoreland* (with an e) and *Devon* were British and three French.

Union Cold Storage acquired *Kaolack* (28) from French owners and, oddly, never changed her name in the eleven years that they owned her. They had also purchased *Britanica* (27) at Buenos Aires for local feeder services along the River Plate. They had also owned an Argentinian subsidiary, Soc. Anon. Frigorifico 'Anglo' for some time but *Britanica* did not join their fleet of two ships, *Anglo No. 1* and *Anglo No. 2*, nor did she change her name.

1925: Two additional sailings per annum were added to the Pacific coast of North America route thereby maintaining an all the year round service. This expansion was fairly insignificant compared with the orders for no fewer than nine ships which was announced in May. The cost of the new vessels was to be £3,500,000—a tremendous sum in those days but trifling when compared with the latest costs involved in the construction of today's specialised fleets. At the time of the order Sir Edmund Vestey made the comment that the keeping of the orders in the British Isles would cost the company some £300,000 when compared with the tenders submitted from abroad but that 'it was in the interests of the country that we should make the sacrifice.'

1926 March saw the launch of *Stuartstar* (30) the first of the extremely large newbuilding programme which, at the time, was one of the largest ever placed by a British shipowner. She was followed at monthly intervals by *Rodneystar* (31) and *Africstar* (32) with the fourth cargo ship, *Napierstar* (33) going down the slipway in August.

Also launched during the year were four of the five 'A' class passenger liners which were planned to have a standard of accommodation equal to, or better than, any that the British, French, Italian or German competition could offer. They were to be First Class-de-luxe. *Almeda* (34), the first of the five, was launched in June to be followed in September by *Andalucia* (35) and *Avila* (38) on consecutive days and on either side of the country—an event which led to much scurrying by the Directors. In December *Avelona* (37) followed to her fitting out berth.

1927 Only four days into the new year *Arandora* (37), the last of the quintet and in some ways the most celebrated, was launched just one month before *Almeda* commenced her acceptance trials. It was to be tragic indeed that during the war that followed not one of the magnificent ships was to survive.

Miltonstar (9) was sold late in the year to Sovtorgflot, Odessa to become their *Dnepr*.

1928 The 'A' class passenger liners had the Admiralty tops to their funnels removed.

1929 In February the Commonwealth & Dominion Line's *Port Albany* was purchased and renamed *Oregonstar* (39). She replaced *Magicstar* which was later sold for £11,500 to the breakers.

Since their introduction in 1927 it had become clear that confusion was arising between the five 'A' of Blue Star and Royal Mail's five 'A' passenger ships *Arlanza*, *Andes*, *Almanzora*, *Asturias* and *Alcantara*.

April: The title of the company was changed to Blue Star Line Ltd by the dropping of the (1920); in addition it was decided to add the word *Star* to the names of the five 'A' and for purposes of conformity to split the names of the other ships in the fleet into two words.

Aug: Two standard 'G' type wartime vessels were acquired from British India S.N. Co and renamed *Fresno Star* (19) and *Tacoma Star* (20); their names reflected their intended service on the North American route. This initiated the practice of allocating names which were directly identifiable with the ships routing. The effect in later years was to give many of the fleet several different names during their careers. Once, however, the reason is understood the name changes become less incoherent.

1930 The Great Depression led to the laying up of some of the older ships for periods of up to two years. The aging *Magicstar*, with no chance of further employment went to the Inverkeithing scrap yard of Thos. W. Ward. With the Atlantic suffering most from the depression Blue Star ships berthed for New Zealand—usually ballasted outbound.

1932 At the Ottawa Conference Great Britain undertook to abandon 'Free Trade' and to give 'Imperial Preference' to the British Dominions and Colonies overseas. This posed a threat to Blue Star's reliance on her Argentine and South American trade. Regular and much increased trade to New Zealand and Australia commenced, initially with much resistance from the established lines. In due course the Company built ships for the trade the design of which called for extensive oil and water bunkers and the cool slow running machinery of the motorship.

1933 *Doric Star* was taken out of service for six months and sent to Jarrow where 60ft (18.29m) of her bow was replaced with a new Maierform section of 90ft (27.43m). Apart from increasing her speed by 1 knot the cargo capacity was also supplemented by an extra hatch served by a pair of derricks. This was the first time that such an operation had been carried out at a British yard.

A service to New Zealand and Australia was inaugurated by *Sultan Star* (40) and *Tuscan Star* (41), both names being unrelated to their service.

1934 During the year and part of the following one, *Almeda Star* (34), *Andalucia Star* (35) and *Avila Star* (38) were withdrawn from service for rebuilding with Maier bows similar to *Doric Star*. Also, in the light of their experience with passenger ships the vessels were extensively refitted and structurally altered.

May: The fire gutted *Oregon Star* (39) arrived at Blyth and was broken up.

Sept: *Saxon Star* (12) and *Roman Star* (13) arrived at Savona within two weeks of each other for demolition.

Oct: *Tudor Star* (5) followed to the same yard.

Nov: *Celtic Star* (16) became the then largest vessel to pass under Tower Bridge to berth at New Fresh Wharf in the Pool of London.

1935 In January the first of a group of four new Harland & Wolff motorships for the 'Down Under' routes entered service when *Imperial Star* (43) was commissioned to be followed two months later by *New Zealand Star* (44) and, in April, came *Australia Star* (45), introducing a poop deck into the series, with the last, *Empire Star* (47), arriving in December. This class of ships, with its later additions, was outstanding and continued, with design modifications, until 1948.

Another acquisition during the year was the old-established shipping concern of Frederick Leyland & Co Ltd. By now they owned no ships but after the purchase a number of Blue Star vessels were transferred but without other outward change.

Five more of the fleet were withdrawn for rebuilding when *Trojan Star* (29), *Stuart Star* (30), *Rodney Star* (31), *Afric Star* (32) and *Napier Star* (33) were modernised. The latter four had their cargo capacity increased by filling in the wells whilst *Trojan Star* had engine modifications aimed at increasing her speed.

1936 February saw the commissioning of *Dunedin Star* (46) by Cammell Laird, Birkenhead with *Sydney Star* (48) arriving from Belfast in March.

1937 A fortunately rare event for the company was the loss by stranding of *Stuart Star* (30) near East London. The spectacle of the huge ship lying close inshore with her back broken became a popular sightseeing outing.

During the year an order was placed with Burmeister & Wain, Copenhagen for three ships. They were sister ships of a design and profile new to the company and became known as the 'C' class. A later fourth ship was to be an addition to the *Dunedin Star* group of 1936. As *Adelaide Star* (53) she never saw company service.

1938 July: *Gothic Star* (10) was broken up as Savona. Burmeister & Wain delivered their first ship, *California Star* (56), to the company and from Lamport & Holt (not yet owned by Blue Star) came *Millais*. She actually appeared in Blue Star colours as *Millais* but was immediately renamed *Scottish Star* (55).

1939 The Danish built pair *Canadian Star* (57) and *Columbia Star* (58) joined the fleet.

Sept 3: At the time of the commencement of the Second World War the fleet of Blue Star stood at 39 ships of almost 400,000 gross tons and in the ensuing five years no fewer than 29 (including one managed *Empire* ship) were to be lost.

The first casualty was, however, a marine hazard when *Ionic Star* (15) went ashore in the Mersey Estuary and became a total loss when the ship broke in two.

Dec 2: *Doric Star* (26) achieved a somewhat bizarre immortality when she became one of the victims of the pocket battleship (actually heavy cruiser) *Admiral Graf Spee* shortly before she was defeated at the battle of the River Plate. It was *Doric Star's* insistent wireless signals that placed the German ship's position off Africa and led to the correct surmise that she would next move towards the River Plate.

1940 Feb 14: In sight of the battle-damaged cruiser *Exeter*, homebound for repairs, *Sultan Star* (40) was sunk by shadowing U-boats one of which was, in turn, claimed sunk by the screening destroyers.

April: *Adelaide Star* (53) was fitting out at Copenhagen when the Germans overran the country. In fact the ship was complete except for some Swedish engine valves. The ship was, in due course, seized and was never to become a unit of the fleet; although she later became prominent because of the litigation that ensued after the war.

June 3: *Avelona Star* (37) was off Cape Finisterre when *U 43* torpedoed her.

June 16: Brand new, the *Wellington Star* (52) had not even completed her maiden round voyage when she was sunk by torpedo.

July 3: *Arandora Star* (36) had survived the evacuations of Narvik, Brest, Quiberon Bay and St. Jean de Luz in a single month. Now loaded with 1,200 Italian and German internees and prisoners of war she was attacked west of Bloody Foreland with the loss of 805 of those aboard her.

July 28: *Wellington Star's* sister ship *Auckland Star* (51) suffered an identical fate towards the end of her first voyage when she fell to an attack by torpedo off Ireland.

Dec 18: The final loss of the year occurred when *Napier Star* (33) became the victim of yet another U-boat torpedo.

1941 Jan 17: The year commenced grievously when the 'A' class passenger liner *Almeda Star* (34) was sunk in severe weather west of the Hebrides. She disappeared without trace of anyone aboard.

Jan 29: *Afric Star* (32) (so often called *Africa Star* in works of reference) was sunk by the raider *Kormoran*.

May: *Rodney Star* (31) was lost by torpedo during an inbound fully laden voyage from Buenos Aires.

July: *Melbourne Star* (49) and *Sydney Star* (48) eached reached Malta safely in convoy.

Sept 27: Not so fortunate was *Imperial Star* (43). She was hit by bombs during a vital Malta convoy dash and had, eventually, to be sunk by her escorting warships. On this occasion *Dunedin Star* (46) got safely through.

1942 The Ministry of War Transport *Empire Galahad*, later to become *Celtic Star* (67) was placed under Blue Star management.

Feb 1: On her way to rendezvous with her convoy to the U.K. *Tacoma Star* (20) was sunk with all hands south of Hampton Roads.

Feb 20: Inbound with her precious cargo *Scottish Star* (55) became the next victim of the U-boat packs.

June 12: Seven days out from Buenos Aires the liner *Avila Star* (38) was blasted twice by torpedo and sank west of the Azores. Her survivors were picked up by the Portuguese warships *Lima* and *Pedro Nunes*; even so 73 lives were lost.

Aug: *Melbourne Star* (49) and *Brisbane Star* (50) were among the five out of 14 merchantmen which reached Malta at the end of 'Operation Pedestal' the most heavily escorted and most ferociously attacked of the Malta convoys. Had they not got through the island would have been starved into submission and, without fuel and ammunition, unable to defend itself.

Aug 25: *Viking Star* (25) was fully laden with frozen meat when she was torpedoed 180 miles south west of Freetown.

Sept 6: *Tuscan Star* (41) was 450 miles out from Freetown on her way home when hit by two torpedoes in quick succession. With a somewhat rare (but by no means unknown) display of chivalry tinned food was passed into the lifeboat containing women and children passengers. The captain of the U-boat explained it by saying that in sinking the ship he was only doing his duty.

Oct 6: *Andalucia Star* (35) was twice torpedoed 200 miles out from Freetown. She was the fifth and the last of the five 'A' class passenger ships; now they had all been sunk in the service of their country. On this occasion all but 7 of those aboard were picked up by the corvette H.M.S. *Petunia*.

Oct 23: Still the frightful toll continued. *Empire Star* (22) bound for Cape Town was sunk in storm conditions while still in mid-Atlantic. The first hit crippled the ship and led to her abandonment but when she remained on a steady keel the U-boat sent two more torpedoes into her and *Empire Star* up ended and sank vertically stern first.

Oct 27: *Pacific Star* (21) was damaged by torpedo and fell behind her convoy but she struggled on towards the nearest land at Las Palmas. After 48 hours the ship lay like a dead log in the water and the crew left her with seas washing over the ship from stem to stern.

Nov 30: As if the terrible carnage caused by war was not enough the final loss of the year came about when *Dunedin Star* (46) struck a submerged object off the dreaded Skeleton Coast and had to be put ashore. The epic of her survivors on shore and their rescue was such that it ended up as a best selling book 'Skeleton Coast' by John H. Marsh.

1943 Mar 4: *California Star* (56) fell victim to a U-boat west of Flores and 51 out of the 74 aboard were lost.

Mar 18: *Canadian Star* (57), a Danish sister to *California Star*, left the United States only days behind the other 'C' class in one of the classic big ship convoys. A battle raged for days between two attacking wolf packs of U-boats during which ten ships were sunk including *Canadian Star*. Such was the mood of the Atlantic for so much of the year that 32 of those who got away from the doomed ship were washed away by the wildness of the sea.

Apr 2: *Melbourne Star* (49) sank like a stone after her torpedo attack. She was laden with ammunition and war supplies and the detonation left the eleven survivors with only life rafts. Four only were rescued from the air 38 days later.

The U-boat war in the Atlantic was now swinging in favour of the Allies, mainly due to the advent of escort aircraft carriers and the closure of the mid-Atlantic gap by the use of aircraft. During the period March-May no fewer than 76 German submarines were sunk.

1944 Apr 21: *Royal Star* (17) which had survived aerial bomb attack in 1941 was this time sunk by aerial torpedo north east of Algiers enroute to Malta. Initially the Captain thought that the vessel might get away with it a second time but after gallant efforts to tow her to safety the first war veteran sank to become the final casualty of the company during the war.

June 5: The old established South American traders Lamport & Holt was acquired on behalf of Blue Star Line by the Union Cold Storage subsidiary Frederick Leyland & Co. This led to an increase in the number of fleet interchanges which can be confusing to the outsider. In effect the old practice of renaming ships to suit their service berth was now extended to include the member of the group operating and crewing the ship. Blue Star commenced to adhere to the system by introducing ships named after the destination cities or states; many of the names were to be new to the company when older revered names—such as *Brisbane Star* and *Sydney Star* were, unaccountably, not to be repeated.

1945 May 8: The end of the war in Europe removed the dreaded threat from the U-boat. Twenty-nine ships had been lost and 646 of the company's personnel had given their lives including 11 masters, 135 deck and engine officers and 500 seamen. (Source Taffrail; other sources give 732 personnel lost).

1946 *Empire Galahad* was renamed *Celtic Star* (67) and *Empire Clarendon* became *Tuscan Star* (66).

The other South American trader Booth Steamship Co was taken over and the interchange of ships extended to include those of the new acquisition.

Two liberty ships of the four 'Sam' bare-boat charters which had been managed by Blue Star were purchased as replacement losses and took the names of *Oregon Star* (63) and *Pacific Star* (64). They were, as their names suggest, employed on the Pacific coast of North America service.

1947 One of the postwar priorities was the re-introduction of the passenge service. The demand was no longer as great and the four new passenger vessels, at 60 berths, carried only one-third of the pre-war ships.

June: *Argentina Star* (70) was delivered. The names, all of South American states, were arranged in alphabetical order of delivery thus *Brasil Star* (71) came next when she was delivered in October.

July: *Fresno Star* (19) went to the Inverkeithing yard of Thos. W. Ward for demolition but *Celtic Star* (67) became one of the many intercompany transfers when she went to Lamport & Holt as *Murillo*.

In Copenhagen the Maritime Court ruled that the non-delivery of *Adelaide Star* (53) in 1940 had been an act of war and that recourse to the Germans should be made to recover the progress payments made.

1948 April: *Albion Star* (18), the company's last surviving World War One standard ship, was broken up at Briton Ferry, South Wales but in the same year the company welcomed no fewer than six new arrivals to expand their depleted fleet. *Paraguay Star* (72) and *Uruguay Star* (73) completed the passenger quartet. Two former escort aircraft carriers had been reconverted into C2 class freighters and became *Rhodesia Star* (76) and *South Africa Star* (77) for the fruit service to Southern Africa and the final pair were straight forward replacements for the highly successful class that had commenced in 1935 with *Imperial Star (I)*; they were *Imperial Star* (74) and *Melbourne Star* (75) honouring two of the Malta convoy stalwarts.

1949 Compagnia Genovese, of Genoa, purchased the 32 year old *Gaelic Star* (16) and, in accordance with their naming tradition, gave her the name *Capo Noli*. To replace her the bare boat chartered *Empire Talisman* became *Tacoma Star* (78).

July 27: The Union Cold Storage Co Ltd changed its name to Union International Co Ltd and the ships which it owned were accordingly re-registered in the name of the new concern. Vestey's did not wish to lose so renowned a name and they retitled (at the next Annual General Meeting) United Cork Industries Ltd to Union Cold Storage. To the onlooker it looked as if the ships were owned by a new company but that was not strictly true.

1950 The ships that had been owned by Frederick Leyland & Co Ltd were transferred to either Blue Star Line or Union International. *Tudor Star* (22), dating from 1919, was broken up at Hendrik-ido Ambracht and *Norman Star* (24) at Blyth. New arrivals were *Adelaide Star* (80), *Dunedin Star* (79), *English Star* (89), *Scottish Star* (90) and *Tasmania Star* (81).

1951 Both the '*Sam*' Liberty ships *Oregon Star* (63) and *Pacific Star* (64) were transferred to Lamport & Holt but Cunard's *Vasconia* was purchased and renamed *Fresno Star* (84) to strengthen the depleted Pacific coast service. Further additions were to be made in the following year.

1952 Austasia Line Ltd was formed, with offices in Singapore, to operate services from there to Malaysian and Australian destinations plus calls at intervening Indonesian ports. Booth's newbuilding *Clement*, was earmarked for the new fleet and was transferred initially to Blue Star (and was launched as *Malay Star* (88)) then to Austasia with the name *Malay*.

Wellington Star (82), the third of the *Adelaide Star* trio was delivered by John Brown & Co, Clydebank. Her cargo capacity, at the time, was the largest in the fleet.

Millais and *Dryden* came across from Lamport & Holt to become *Oregon Star* (III) (68) and *Freemantle Star* (87) respectively.

Sir Edmund Vestey, Bart, died during 1952.

1953 *Memling* followed her sister *Millais* and was renamed *Vancouver Star* (86).

1954 In June the Glasgow based Donaldson Line disposed of its services and assets to the Pacific Coast of North America and Blue Star Line took them over including the three wartime standard ships employed. *Carmia* became *Victoria Star* (85), *Gracia* replaced *Oregon Star* (III), which had just been sold, and entered the fleet as *Oregon Star* (IV) (96); this ship, although a standard ship, differed in profile from her consorts. The third vessel involved was *Corrientes*; she was earmarked for renaming to *Oakland Star* but being surplus to requirements was sold to Williamson & Co, Hong Kong, to become *Inchmay*. Lamport & Holt's *Delius* and *Delane* were brought across to amplify the expanded service and became *Portland Star* (97) and *Seattle Star* (98); while *Defoe* was transferred to the Australian route as *Geelong Star* (94).

One inexplicable purchase during the year was Heyn's *North Down* which came to Blue Star as *Drover* (93) and lasted but one month before passing to the Belfast SS Co as *Ulster Herdsman*. There was nothing suspect about the ship herself because she lasted a further eleven years.

Another oddity was the group's essay into tanker owning with the building of *Pacific Star* (95) for Booth SS Co with Blue Star as bare-boat charterers. She holds the distinction of being the group's only traditional tanker.

The move into pure 'Reefer' ownership commenced with the purchase of *Mosdale* which lasted mere days in Blue Star Line colours as *Albion Star* (91) before transitting to Lamport & Holt as *Balzac*. Six years later she was to come back.

1955 May: *Trojan Star* (29), the oldest vessel in the fleet, was broken up at Blyth.

Her final voyage had been full of incidents all of which pointed clearly to the fact that the grand old lady had reached the end of her days.

Victoria Star joined the Williamson fleet as *Inchean*; she was young enough to last with them until 1966. *Barfleur*, virtually a sister of *Norman Star* (II) (91) also has a very brief spell with Blue Star as *Roman Star* before passing on to Booth Line as *Bede* who, not exactly in exchange, parted with *Devis* which became *Oakland Star* (99); an unrefrigerated ship, her first assignment was to Belfast for the installation of Reefer plant as did her consort *Washington Star* (100).

1956 Five vessels were built in Germany at Bremen-Vegesack, amid much comment in the British shipping press. *Canberra Star* (101) entered service first followed by *Newcastle Star* (102) and then *Hobart Star* (103).

1957 The final, longer fcsled, pair of German built ships *Gladstone Star* and *Townsville Star* (104/5) were commissioned and two existing ships *Tacoma Star* (78) and *Fresno Star* (84) reappeared in the black, white and blue Lamport & Holt as *Murillo* and *Millais*. For the northern deepwater ports of Australia *Queensland Star* and *Rockhampton Star* (106/7) were commissioned; they, like so many Blue Star ships possessed both 'freeze' and 'chill' compartments. For the Canadian route what more appropriate ship than *Canadian Star* (108) a one-off design from Caledon in Dundee.

Crusader Shipping Co Ltd was formed in partnership with New Zealand Shipping Co, Port Line (Cunard group) and Shaw, Savill & Albion. Their first vessel was purchased on the stocks and was completed as *Crusader* for a service between New Zealand and Japan. As the company became established ships from the partner's fleets were chartered and bore Crusader livery.

1958 The additions of *Auckland Star* (83) a fourth unit of the *Adelaide Star* (II) class completed after a gap of 8 years and *Rockhampton Star* (107) brought the post war fleet to forty vessels thereby surpassing the 39 owned at the outbreak of war in 1939. With justification the mail from the London Head Office was franked with the words 'Blue Star Line services span the world'.

1959 Blue Star Line laid down a feeder vessel but in the event the ship emerged as *Siddons* for Lamport & Holt.

Ulster Star (111), which had no sisters, was commissioned for general services and the year's disposal was *Vancouver Star* (86) which had been transferred from L & H six years earlier.

1960 Five sisterships—except for the substitution of cranes in the last pair—were ordered from Bartrams. They were smaller ships than most of the long-haul fleet and were designed to service the secondary ports in Australasia as well as having the flexibility to serve on the North American routes. *Canterbury Star* (I) (112/114) was the lead vessel. Another delivery was *Fremantle Star* by Cammell Laird. The banana carrier *Norman Star* (91), once briefly registered as *Albion Star*, re-appeared in Blue Star colours but once more her stay was to be short because in 1961 she moved to Booth Line as *Basil*.

1961 A further two wartime standard ships were sold; *Nelson Star* (60) which left the service of the company to become *Eirini* and *Saxon Star* (61) renamed *Redbrook*. A third wartime building, *Tacoma Star* (78), was scrapped at Vigo.

The only oil tanker ever owned by the group, *Pacific Star* (95) was sold after only seven years in the fleet. Even though she preceded the era of VLCCs she was nevertheless too small to enjoy economic operation. That this facet had been apparent for some time is borne out by the fact that she was never duplicated.

1962 A 24-days-at-sea service was introduced between Australia and east coast ports of the United States and Canada terminating at Montreal in summer and Halifax, Nova Scotia in winter.

Townsville Star took the inaugural sailing.

Oregon Star (68) was dismantled in the Netherlands and *Seattle Star* (98) at Hong Kong.

From Lamport & Holt came *Santos Star* (118/9) and *Mendoza Star* for the South America-Mediterranean service terminating in Italy. The results were promising that in the following year they were jumboised.

1963 The Hoboken yard of S. A. Cockerill-Ougree lengthened *Santos Star* and *Mendoza Star* increasing their cargo capacity by 1,000 tons. *Montreal Star* (113) became the first custom built ship for the Antipodes—North America route.

Booth's *Anselm* was transferred to become *Iberia Star* (120) thereby increasing to five—as in pre-war days—the number of passenger ships on the South American service. The move to some extent removed surplus Booth capacity on their Liverpool—Manaus ('1,000 miles up the Amazon') route but *Iberia Star* was only to occupy the berth for two years before being seconded to the Austasia Line.

1964 *America Star* (114) and *Halifax Star* (115) joined *Montreal Star* on the East coast service and *Townsville Star* was re-registered with Lamport & Holt as owners but without other change.

The Mediterranean Reefer business from South America was extended by the purchase of two of Africanische Frucht Cie's fruit carriers which entered service as *Padova Star* (122) and (1965) *Barcelona Star* (123). The other Reefer purchase came from Norway's Olsen & Ugelstad to be renamed *Genova Star* (121).

June: Feeder services to support main line ships feature in the histories of many companies, often reaching considerable proportions as seen in the Blue Funnel Line's Singapore operations. Blue Star had used the tactic in the past both in the River Plate area and at Madagascar. *Britanica* (27) had also served out of London to near Continental ports. Now two small ships, *Waveney Star* and *Orwell Star* (124/5) were put into the Continental ports feeder service. The truth of the adage that big ship and small ship operation do not mix still lay in future. During June *Australia Star* (45) was scrapped at Faslane.

Sept: An agreement was reached whereby Blue Star and the German concern Columbus Schiffahrts GmbH pooled their services to enable the Australia—East Coast to North America sailings to become two-weekly in place of monthly.

1965 For the purposes of expanding the Italian reefer trade Calmedia S.p.A di Nav. was formed at Cagliari, Sardinia by Blue Star and Italian shippers. The five ships employed between South America and Italy were progressively transferred to the new concern (mostly early in 1966) and given names commencing with the prefix *Cala*. *Barcelona Star* (123) was the first to be renamed; she became *Calasetta*.

Oct: *Brisbane Star* (50) was broken up at Osaka and during the same month the salvaged *Napier Star* (62), lying at Montevideo, was declared a constructive total loss.

A replacement *Australia Star* (128) was delivered by Austin & Pickersgill a ship having the distinction of carrying the heaviest single-derrick afloat—one capable of lifting 300 tons. The advent of heavy lift gear had come with *South Africa Star* which had been equipped in 1963 with a 120 ton lift derrick but the plans to equip her sistership with even larger equipment had been cancelled and plans for *Australia Star* substituted.

Austasia Line took delivery of *Iberia Star* (ex *Anselm*) and placed her in service as *Australasia*.

1966 Jan 12: The first Board Meeting of Associated Container Transportation Ltd (A.C.T.) was held in London. The subscribing members comprised five of Britain's most prominent shipping companies. In addition to Blue Star Line the partners consisted of the Ben Line Steamers Ltd (Wm. Thomson & Co), the Cunard Steamship Co Ltd (who vested their operation in their subsidiary the Port Line Ltd), Ellerman Lines Ltd and Thos. & Jas. Harrison's Charente Steam-Ship Co Ltd.

The first service was to be from U.K./Europe-Australia.

Work commenced to establish the company and to design and construct their first vessels—a period which was to occupy three years.

In A.C.T. the partners recognised the revolutionary aspect of containerisation. The economies in ship operation were coupled with the increase in the speed of delivery on a door-to-door basis. Damage and theft were reduced and manufacturers were able to pack and control their products in a manner hitherto undreamed of.

Perhaps, at the time, it was not foreseen just how speedily this new type of specialist ship would out-date the modern conventional cargo carrier. Yet within a decade the advent of containerisation was to spread across the globe to bring about the greatest technological advance since the coming of motive power at sea.

In 1966 *Catalina Star* (87) reverted to Lamport & Holt as *Devis*, *Santos Star*, *Genova Star* and *Padova Star* joined *Barcelona Star* in Calmedia colours and were renamed.

Sept: Kaohsiung saw the arrival of *Fresno Star* (84) where she joined the motley collection of ships anchored in the bay waiting their turn to be towed into the scrap yards.

One of the other re-organisational moves was placement of the feeder ships under the management of the long established coaster operators G. T. Gillie & Blair Ltd and the dropping of the word *Star* from their names although Blue Star colours were retained. To *Waveney* and *Orwell* were added new sisters *Crouch* (126/7) and *Deben*.

1967 March: *South Africa Star* (77), the C.2 type former escort carrier was scrapped in Japan.

June 4: saw *Scottish Star* (90) trapped with 14 others in the Great Bitter Lake of the Suez Canal (with one lone ship in Lake Timseh) by the Arab-Israeli war. Little did anyone know that the ship would spend 8 years, almost to the day, at anchor.

July: *New Zealand Star* (44) dating from 1935, was finally broken up at Kure. She was replaced by a second *New Zealand Star* and sistership *Southland Star* (130/31) released *Sydney Star* (48) for breaking up. Blue Star Port Lines (Management) Ltd was formed to operate the joint working of the Australasian interests of both. The unit quickly became known as Blue Port.

Also during 1967 the final part of Donaldson's routage—the Glasgow—South American sector—was absorbed by Blue Star and Donaldson's went into voluntary liquidation.

1968 Nov: *Columbia Star* (58) ended her varied career under four different names within the group when she arrived for demolition at Kaohsiung. Another move was the transfer of *Dunedin Star* (79)—the one non-Blue Star profile in the fleet—to Lamport & Holt as *Roland* who at this juncture were giving all their fast units names beginning with 'R'. The run down of the feeder service ships commenced with the sale of *Orwell*.

1969 Mar 22: *ACT 1* sailed for Australia on her maiden voyage.

Apr: *California Star* (66) was scrapped in the Far East.

Aug: *Paraguay Star* (73), one of the four remaining passenger liners, suffered severe fire damage while berthed at the Royal Victoria Dock, London. At her age repairs were not worthwhile and after being condemned as beyond repair she was towed to Hamburg for breaking up. Because, too, of declining passenger demand in competition with air travel no attempt was made to replace her.

1970 A survey of shipbuilding recorded the costs of refrigeration in ships. A dry cargo vessel of 15,000 dwt cost £2½ million. The same ship fully refrigerated cost £3 million more; mainly because the holds have to be in separated chambers capable of being maintained at the cold temperature, most suitable to the range of products being carried—a range going from 'chilled' to 'deep freeze'. Some saving can accrue if specialised ships are built for specialised trades—like bananas—but the price is a loss of flexibility.

Waveney was sold for further trading.

1971 *California Star* (III) (132) and *Columbia Star* (II) (133) introduced containerisation on the North America Pacific route. The service was in conjunction with the Copenhagen firm East Asiatic Co and bore the name ScanStar.

Sept: *Imperial Star* (74), built in 1948, was scrapped.

Oct: *Empire Star* (59), the finest specimen of wartime building when completed as *Empire Mercia* was broken up. She spent the years from 1950 onwards owned by Lamport & Holt but never changed her name or colours and now arrived in Taiwan.

Dec: Another wartime vessel *Caledonia Star* (65) ended a group career of 29 years at Kaohsuing.

During the year the final pair of feeder ships, *Crouch* and *Deben* were disposed of.

1972 May: The ScanStar consortium was joined by Axel Johnson to form Johnson ScanStar. The fleet consisted of 5 Johnson vessels, 2 Blue Star and 2 East Asiatic container ships. A weekly departure planned Gothenburg—Continental Europe—US Pacific ports—Vancouver and return in 63 days. Greenock—Los Angeles requires only 15 days.

As part of the extension of container work *America Star*, *Halifax Star* and *New York Star* (114/116) went to Sandfjord in Norway to be jumboised before returning to the Australia—East Coast of North America service.

Canadian Star (108) was transferred to Lamport & Holt as *Raeburn* and *Colorado Star* (109) moved across to serve under Austasia colours as *Mahsuri*.

Passenger services to South America were finally terminated after 45 years with the disposal of *Argentina Star*, *Brasil Star* and *Uruguay Star* (70/72) to Taiwan breakers. They were replaced by four cargo-only motorships three of whose names were changed to reflect the destination served. *Newcastle Star* emerged as *Montevideo Star* (102) *Queensland Star* was renamed *Brasilia Star* (106) and *Hobart Star* which became *Buenos Aires Star* (103) for a single voyage before being withdrawn following collision damage and reverting to her original name. The gap was filled by *Canberra Star* which took the name *Buenos Aires Star* (101). The fourth member of the group was *Ulster Star* (111) whose name remained.

In August *Melbourne Star* (75) was sold to Embajada Cia Nav. who loaded her with a final cargo before being traded to a scrap dealer.

1973 *English Star* (89) arrived in Taiwan for demolition but *Australia Star* (128), of the heavy derrick, was sold for further trading.

1974 A survey in June revealed that out of a world total of 1,212 Reefer vessels of 8,562,000 gross tons Great Britain had the largest number 158 of 1,610,669 grt more than twice that of any other country. Blue Star was the leading British operator with 23 'reefers' (a ship with all holds refrigerated).

In the spring of the year Blue Star Ship Management was formed to husband the ships of Blue Star Line, Lamport & Holt and Booth S.S. Co. The old White Star Line headquarters at Albion House, Liverpool was acquired for the purpose and the supply stores and depots established.

1975: Jan: Blue Star Ship Management became operational from Albion House, Liverpool.

Feb: *Afric Star* (134) became the first of six 'A' class of Reefers; she was registered as being owned by Glencairn Shipping Co on bare-boat charter to Blue Star. She was followed in June by *Avila Star* then *Andalucia Star* (135/6), whose maiden event was to berth in the Pool of London so that Head Office staff and guests could see her.

Mar: The twenty-five year old *Adelaide Star* (80) suffered such severe engine room damage that the ship was adjudged to be beyond repair and broken up; her sister *Tasmania Star* (81) was taken out of service later in the year.

1976 *Almeria Star* of the 'A' class was delivered, her name replaced that of the much venerated *Arandora Star* which of the original five passenger liners was the only one not to be repeated. (The sixth 'A' *Afric Star* (II) was the lead ship of the four cargo vessels built during the famed 1927 nine ship order). She was followed by the final pair *Almeda Star* (II) and *Avelona Star* (II).

For the 'banana trade' two of the bankrupt fleet of Maritime Fruit Carriers were acquired to become *Tuscan Star* (140) and *Trojan Star* (141). *Montevideo Star* (102) was disposed of and broken up.

1978 Australia Star (142), the first two container ships for the Australia and New Zealand service was commissioned. Her sister *New Zealand Star* (143) was launched in July.

1979 To make way for the new ship of the name *New Zealand Star* (130) was renamed *Wellington Star*.

Nov: *Brasilia Star* (106) built at Govan as *Queensland Star* ended her days when she left Newhaven for the last time.

Avila Star (II) was sold to Kornelius Olsen for further trading and remains in their service.

1980 *Townsville Star* (105) was scrapped in Taiwan.

Cochin, India, became port of call for containerships.

1981 *Rockhampton Star* (107) was sold for further trading but was broken up within year.

1982 July: Trade with the Argentine was severed by the invasion of the Falkland Islands. The British Government soon thereafter chartered *Andalucia Star* (136) and *Avelona Star* (139) for supply ship service; each had a helicopter pad fitted aft. They bore funnels with the red portion and star painted white.

America Star (114) was sold for further trading.

1983 Four ships were ordered from Harland & Wolff, Belfast and they had the distinction of all being built in the massive drydock at the same time.

Oct: *Halifax Star* (115) was scrapped in China.

1984 Dec: Fire broke out in the engine room of the nearly complete *English Star* (145) fitting out at Harland & Wolff. The damage caused amounted to over £1 million and delivery of the ship was postponed by at least six months. Work on the second ship *Scottish Star* was immediately accelerated.

1985 Jan 25: H.R.H. the Duchess of Kent, accompanied by Chairman Edmund Vestey, performed the naming ceremony of *English Star* (II). By coincidence it was virtually 25 years since *Ulster Star* (III) was built in 1959 and fifty years since *Imperial Star* (43), Harland & Wolff's first ship for Blue Star, was completed in 1935.

Mar: *Scottish Star* (144) was delivered to become the first of the four ships into service.

The advent of the four ships will release, at the end of their five year charter period the four Sasebo built ships.

Four of the five remaining 'A' class were sold to companies in the Hong Kong based Wallem group. Thus after ten years service *Andalucia Star*, *Almeria Star*, *Almeda Star* (II) and *Avelona Star* (II) (136-139) left the fleet.

1986 Excepting the chartered vessels the fleet now comprised ten ships. They were:

Afric Star (134), *Auckland Star* (146), *Australia Star* (142), *California Star* (132), *Canterbury Star* (147), *Columbia Star* (133), *English Star* (145), *Scottish Star* (144), *Southland Star* (129) and *Wellington Star* (130).

The BHLR service (Blue Star, Houlder, Lamport & Holt and Royal Mail) was renamed the Brisa (Spanish for Breeze) Service for ease of marketing. The four members then formed the new Joint Container Service Consortium in conjunction with Hamburg Sud-Amerika, Alianca, Cie Maritime Belge, Havenlijn, SEAS (D'Orbigny), Rotterdam Zuid-Amerika and Nedlloyd. A fleet totalling nine ships was placed on the South American routes. Late in the year *Afric Star* was sold and *Columbia Star* transferred to Austasia being given the name *Mandama*.

A new venture commenced when the Falkland Island squid fishing industry was served by a Blue Star chartered vessel, the *Perseus* (ex-Cunard's *Carmania*) to operate Falklands—Japan.

To deal with break bulk container bookings from the west coast of Canada a Vancouver office was opened. In addition Lion Shipping Ltd, Hong Kong was formed to manage seven locally owned reefers.

1987 *Calfornia Star* (132) was transferred to Austasia as *Mulbera*—a distinguished name from the days of British India.

1988 The owned fleet stands at seven: *Canterbury Star* (147), *Horncliff* (*Auckland Star* on charter (146), *Hornsea* (*English Star* on charter) (145), *Scottish Star* (144), *Southland Star* (129) and *Wellington Star* (130). Associated Containers own three *ACT 1*, *ACT 5* and *ACT 7*. While Lamport & Holt operate *Churchill* (ex *New Zealand Star* (143)). In addition *Leif Hoegh* (Leif Hoegh & Co A.S.) is only manned by BSSM crew. Blue Star Line still charters extra tonnage to meet its needs. The Vancouver serving vessel *Lairg* is group owned but operated by the Merlion Singapore subsidiary.

Finally, late this year, Albion House will be vacated as the thriving organisation transfers to new custom designed premises in the revitalised docklands area.

ROUTES

Many of the dates are approximate because of service variations.

1909-1985 Cargo. Liverpool/London—South American ports terminating at Buenos Aires. Enroute calls have varied between Maderia, Las Palmas, Tenerife (Puerto de la Cruz) and Lisbon.
1911-1930 Periodically. U.K.—Hong Kong—Shanghai—(occasionally) Japan.
1915-1920 London—Tenerife—Cape Town—Majunga.
1920-1985 U.K.—Panama Canal—North Pacific coast ports of U.S.A. and Canada.
1927-1972 Passenger. London—Boulogne—Lisbon—Madeira—Tenerife/Las Palmas—Rio de Janeiro—Santos—Montevideo—Buenos Aires.
1933-1985 U.K.—Panama Canal—New Zealand ports.
1934-1985 U.K.—Suez Canal—Singapore—Australian ports.
1934-1985 U.K.—Panama Canal—Australian ports.
1935-1985 U.K.—South African ports.
1936 Avonmouth was added as a U.K. port of call.
1938-1985 U.K.—West Indies.
1946-1985 U.K.—Suez Canal—New Zealand—Persian Gulf—Middle East ports—Suez Canal—U.K.
1946-1972 Glasgow—South Africa—Australia.
1962-1985 Australia—Panama Canal—East coast ports of U.S.A. and Canada, terminating at Montreal.
1964-1966 River Plate—Barcelona—Marseilles—Genoa/Italian ports.
1964-1970 Continental ports—London feeder service.
1965-1970 Tyne—Middlesbrough—Humber—London feeder services.
1971-1985 ScanStar and Johnson ScanStar container service. Gothenburg—Copenhagen—Liverpool—Clyde—Panama Canal—Los Angeles—Seattle—Vancouver with some calls at Oakland.
1972-1985 World wide reefer tramping according to season. Blue Star has also chartered into its fleet a number of smaller container ships which have increased the number of ports of call on their traditional routings.
1972-1985 New Zealand ports direct—Los Angeles—Oakland—Seattle—Vancouver.
1976-1985 Containers: Port Chalmers—New Plymouth—Melbourne—Fremantle—Muscat—Dubai—Damman—Kuwait—Khorramshahr—Bandar Shahpur. In 1980 Cochin, India, was added.

LIVERY

During its history the company introduced variants which were not applied universally across the fleet nor were any changes made simultaneously.

Funnels	**1909-1910**	Vestey Bros. Pink-buff and black top. Viz: Shaw Savill & Albion colours.
	1910-1911	Plain buff, black top with a blue star on the buff.
	1912-1920	Blue Star Line Ltd. Pillar box red, black top. White disc with a 5 pointed blue star in the centre.
	1920-1985	Orange-red with black top thin white and black bands touching the black top, white disc and blue star in the centre. (See front cover). The white band in nearly all cases has been a fraction thicker than the adjoining black band. In recent years the white has become twice as broad.
Hulls	**1909-1959**	Black. When, in 1959, dove grey was introduced it was not universal. Some ships, the general cargo vessels, retained black hulls throughout their careers.
	1959-1985	All newbuildings were given grey hulls. Reefers: white.
	1960	Experimental lavender existed but was short lived.
	1927-1939	White hull bands were painted at main deck level but not in the case of the five passenger ships which had white painted fcsles, bridge deck and poop.
	1945-1985	The white band did not reappear after the war; ships had white painted forecastles, bridge decks and poops. This practice continued when grey hulls were introduced. The reefers and Mediterranean fleet had white hulls.
Waterline	**1909-1911**	Red.
	1912-1914	Red, white dividing line. These apparently were a left over from the second hand vessels which already sported the white dividing line. In 1927 the passenger ships were given a white dividing line between the red and the black of the hull.
	1920-1959	Red.
	1959-1975	Dark blue in ships with grey or white hulls. Red remained for black hulled ships.
	1975-1985	Black or dark blue with red below the waterline.
Uppers & Lifeboats	**1909-1985**	White. 1956-7 Newbuildings had brown boats but not for long.
	1927-1939	Some of the general cargo ships were given stone-brown uppers and lifeboats.
Decks	**1975**	Grey-green.
Masts	**1909-1960**	Biscuit buff.
	1961-1985	Light grey king posts, derricks and deck cranes with white masting. This included ships which retained black hulls. Reefers and Mediterranean ships: white.

Note: Chartered ships kept their own colours except for the Blue Star funnel.

Fleet Index

Illustrated Fleet List

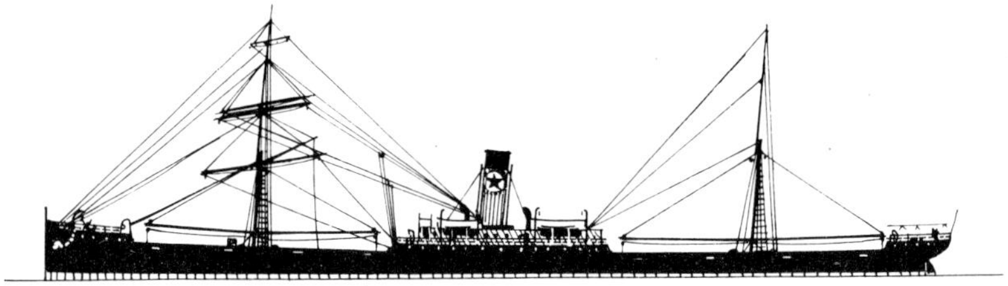

LIZANKA/BRODERICK, BRODMORE

1 **LIZANKA/BRODERICK**
B1890 R. Ropner & Son, Stockton-on-Tees. **T** 4,331g, 2,842n.
D 364.8ft (111.19m) x 47 (14.32) x 26.9 (8.2).
E Sgl scr, tpl exp, 3 cyls, 415 NHP, 10 kts. 2 dbl ended blrs, Stm P:160lb.
By Blair & Co, Stockton.
H Steel. 2 dks. F 38 (11.58). B 88 (26.82). P 23 (7.01).
1890 June 19: Launched as *Pakeha* for Shaw Savill & Albion and registered at Southampton. Aug: Delivered.
1909 Sept 18: Acquired by Vestey Brothers and r/n *Lizanka*, London. At this time there was no ship owning structure and the first ships were therefore registered by individuals on the Vestey Board who in turn signed the necessary relinquishing document in favour of the true owners. This was a fairly common practice and accounts for many of the 'one off' names to be found in Lloyd's Registers. In this case the name was William P. Outram.
1910 Oct: Chartered for one year to the Russian Ministry of Fisheries, Vladivostok, to act as a mother ship to the Siberian salmon fishing fleet. Manager E. E. Rulcovius. Because of winter ice the first part of the charter was the delivery of the prior season's catch.
1911 Sept: With the ending of the Siberian season and the charter she was returned to Vestey's (and W. P. Outram). Her name was changed to *Broderick* and ownership was Broderick S.S. Co, London.
1912 Jan: The newly formed Blue Star Line Ltd was appointed managers.
1918 Apr 29: Torpedoed by *UB-57* 7 miles off Hastings enroute London—Puerto Cabello, Venezuela with a general cargo.

2 **BRODMORE**
Details as *Broderick* except **B** 1890 Wm Gray, West Hartlepool. **T** 4,045g, 2,642n. **D** 365/111.25. **B** By Central Marine Eng Co, West Hartlepool.
1890 June 6: Launched as *Rangatira* for Shaw, Savill & Albion. Aug: Completed. She had a taller and thinner funnel than her sister.
1909 Sept 18: Acquired by Vestey Brothers.
1910 Oct: Joined her sister on the Vladivostok berth for six months. R/n *Count Muravieff*, the then Minister. Same manager although by the end of the period the name was J. M. Eriksen and her name appears as *Count Murajev* although the cyrillic spelling for both remains the same. Used to deliver the season's catch and did not serve in north Siberian waters.
1911 May: Became *Brodmore*. Mark Hinchliff and then Josiah Ragg were listed until Brodmore S.S. Co was formed, with them as directors, to operate her.
1912 Transferred to Blue Star Line Ltd as managers.
1917 Feb 27: Torpedoed by *UB-43* 70 miles north-west of Marsa Susa, North Africa enroute Majunga—UK with frozen meat. Her master was taken prisoner aboard the submarine.

BRODLAND

3 **BRODLAND**
B 1891 Craig Taylor & Co, Stockton-on-Tees. **T** 2,989g, 1,949n.
D 310ft (94.49m) x 41.2 (12.56) x 17.8 (5.42).
E Sgl scr, tpl exp, 3 cyls 272 NHP, 9 kts. 2 sgl ended blrs Stm P: 160lb. By Westgarth, English & Co, Middlesbrough.
H Steel. 1 dk + spar dk. F 41 (12.49). B 80 (24.38). P 37 (11.28).
1891 Apr 9: Launched. July: Delivered to the Nelson Line, H & W Nelson managers, as *Highland Mary*; one of three sisters by different yards. Single ship company owned.
1900 Consolidated into Nelson Line (Liverpool) Ltd. Same managers.
1912 Jan: Became *Brodland*, Brodland S.S. Co, London, with Blue Star Line as managers. Feb 1: She made Blue Star's first official sailing; it was from Barry Dock, South Wales, with coal for Buenos Aires.
1913 Jan 20: Wrecked on Aberavon beach during a south-westerly gale enroute Port Talbot—Punta Arenas with coal. The whole crew were rescued by Breeches Bouy.

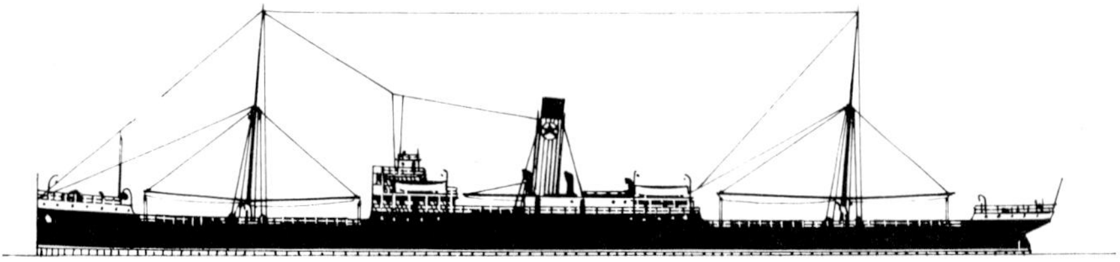

BRODSTONE

4 **BRODSTONE (I)**
B 1896 Chas. Connell & Co, Scotstoun, Glasgow. **T** 4,927g, 3,181n.
D 400.4ft (122.04m) x 48.2 (14.69) x 29 (8.84).
E Sgl scr, tpl exp, 3 cyls, 485 NHP, 10 kts. Stm P: 200lb. By D. Rowan & Sons, Glasgow.
H Steel. 2 dks. F 50 (15.24). B 135 (41.15). P 29 (8.84).
1896 March 5: Launched as *Indraghiri* for Thos. B. Royden's Indra Line, Liverpool. Owned by the single ship company of the same name.
1910 Nov: Purchased by Vestey Bros and renamed *Brodstone*. She was the first vessel in the fleet to bear the prefix *Brod*. Managed by William Outram. (*Lizanka* and *Brodmore* were not renamed until they rejoined the fleet in 1911.)
1912 Blue Star Line Ltd were appointed managers, the ship being owned by Brodstone S.S. Co. Her first voyage for the company was from Barry Dock, with coal, to Shanghai were a cargo of frozen pork was to be lifted. The venture was not a success and only one voyage was made before *Brodmore* was placed on the River Plate service.
1915 Used as a food transport for the British Expeditionary Force in France.
1917 Aug 15: Torpedoed by *UB-40* 100 miles west of Ushant enroute Cardiff—Zarate, Argentine. Five crewmen killed.

BRODVALE/TUDORSTAR/TUDOR STAR (I)

5 **BRODVALE/TUDORSTAR/TUDOR STAR (I)**
B 1899 Sir James Laing & Sons, Sunderland. **T** 5,987g, 3,906n.
D 440 (134.11) x 54.3 (16.55) x 29 (8.84).
E Sgl scr, tpl exp, 3 cyls, 515 NHP, 11 kts. 3 dbl ended blrs. Stm P: 160lb. By G. Clark, Sunderland.
H Steel. 2 dks. Flush decker.
Identification: Unlike the other five ships with similar outlines *Brodvale* had a flush bridge front and no projecting deck or housing.
1899 March 11: Launched as *Tomoana* for Tyser & Co. Owned by Tomoana S.S. Co.
June 16: M/v London—Australia.
1903 The owners became Tyser Line Ltd.
1912 Acquired and renamed *Brodvale*, owned by Brodvale S.S. Co, Blue Star as managers. **T** 6,837g.
1920 Transferred to Blue Star (1920) Ltd as managers but owned by Union Cold Storage Co Ltd. Renamed *Tudorstar*.
1922 Dec 19: The bridge work was washed away during a severe Atlantic gale and a great deal of flooding took place. Other ships stood by as *Tudorstar* lay heaved to. Eventually Greenock was reached on December 28.
1929 Renamed *Tudor Star* when all the one worded named were split into two.
1934 Oct 6: Arrived at Savona, Italy, for breaking up by S. A. Ricuperi Metallici. She had been laid up all year.

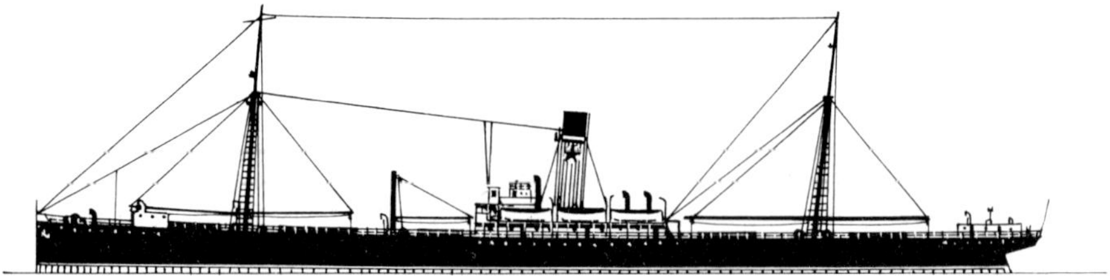

BRODMOUNT/STUARTSTAR (I) BRODLIFFE/TUSCANSTAR

6 **BRODMOUNT/STUARTSTAR (I)**
B 1899 R. & W. Hawthorn Leslie & Co, Hebburn-on-Tyne. **T** 5,706g, 3,071n.
D 420ft (128.02m) x 54 (16.46) x 28 (8.72).
E Sgl scr, tpl exp, 3 cyls, 491 NHP, 11 kts. 3 sgl ended blrs. Stm P: 160 lb. By builder.
H Steel. 2 dks, well deck aft covered. F & B 355 (108.2). P 50 (15.24).
C 221,280 cu ft (6,266 cu m) refrigerated.
1898 Nov 15: Launched as *Wakanui* for the New Zealand Shipping Co, London but, like all their pre-1939 ships, registered at Plymouth. Her sisters were *Waimate* and *Whakatane*.
1899 Feb: Entered service London—New Zealand.
1913 Apr: Acquired for £40,000 and renamed *Brodmount*, owned by Brodmount S.S. Co with Blue Star Line as managers.
1919 Reboilered.
1920 Renamed *Stuartstar*, managed by Blue Star (1920) Ltd but now owned by Union Cold Storage.
1923 Oct 4: Enroute Zarate—Rotterdam the ship blew ashore at the Hook of Holland and was abandoned when she broke her back. After some weeks the wreck was pronounced a danger to navigation and demolished by explosives. Cargo: Frozen meat, much of which salvaged and destroyed.

7 **BRODLIFFE/TUSCANSTAR**
Sister to 6 except: **B** 1898. **T** 5,464g, 3,505n.
1898 Sept 1: Launched as the *Morayshire* for Elderslie S.S. Co, Glasgow. One of the Turnbull Martin Group. Dec: Delivered.
1900 Made three produce voyages from Australia to South Africa as a Boer War supply ship.
1910 Ownership transferred to the Scottish Shire Line.
1911 Collided with the Thames collier *Axwell* in Lower Hope and sank her. *Morayshire* was adjudged to have been on the wrong side of the stream.
1915 March: Became *Brodliffe*, Brodliffe S.S. Co with Blue Star Line as managers.
1917 Apr 3: Missed by U-boat torpedo.
1920 April: Renamed *Tuscanstar* and owned by Union Cold Storage with Blue Star (1920) Ltd as managers. Photographs exist bearing her name as *Tuscan Star*.
1929 Jan: Sold for £11,500 to G. & S. Rizzuto, Italy; renamed *Fortunestar*.
1936 Purchased by Ignacio Messina Cia and renamed *Semien*. White hulled.
1942 After fire damage had been repaired the Swiss Nautilus S.A. took the ship over as a neutral safe conduct food ship for Swiss nationals. They renamed her *Lugano*; white hull yellow funnel with both Red Cross and Swiss emblems on the flanks and funnel.
1948 Reverted to Messina ownership; placed on the South America meat service.
1952 July 30: Arrived at Savona for demolition.

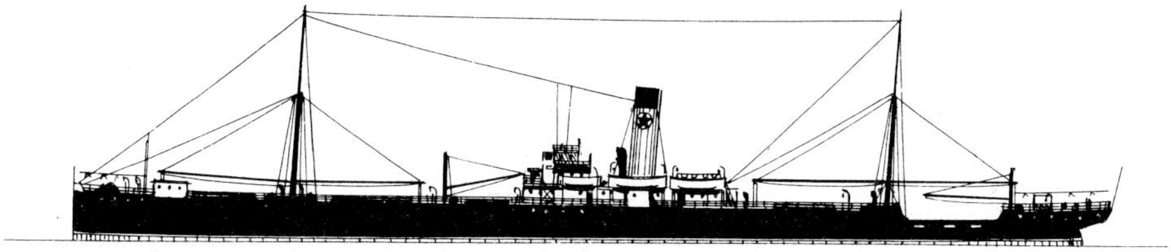

BRODNESS

8 BRODNESS
Sister to *Brodmount* (6) except: **T** 5,537g, 3,584n.
H F. & B. 344 (104.85). P 41 (12.5).
1894 Sept 1: Launched as *Banffshire* for Elderslie S.S. Co. Nov: Completed.
1910 Ownership transferred to Turnbull Martin & Co's Scottish Shire Line. Same name.
1915 June: Acquired with her sister. R/n *Brodness*, Brodness S.S. Co with Blue Star Line as managers.
1917 Mar 31: Torpedoed off Anzio, Bay of Naples, enroute Genoa—Port Said. The submarine was Austro-Hungarian and had evaded the Taranto Strait net barrage. Both *U-3* and *U-6* claimed the sinking.

BRODHURST/MILTONSTAR

9 BRODHURST/MILTONSTAR
B 1914 Clyde SB & Eng. Works, Port Glasgow. **T** 3,071g, 2,109n, 5,570dwt.
D 304.3ft (92.75m) x 44.7 (13.63) x 27.2 (8.29).
E sgl scr, tpl exp, 3 cyl, 1,460 NHP, 9½ kts. By builder. Steaming radius 3,580 miles.
H Steel. 1 + shelter dk. C 152,800 cu ft (4,326cu m) refrig.
1914 Oct 31: Launched as *Yula* for W. H. Stott's Stott (Baltic) Steamers Ltd. Acquired on the stocks and r/n *Brodhurst*, Brodland S.S. Co. Blue Star Line as managers. This was the first newbuilding owned by Blue Star but not the first actually to be built for them.
1915 Jan: following the loss of the parent ship the owners became Brodhurst S.S. Co.
1920 Oct: R/n *Miltonstar* with Union Cold Storage Ltd as owners; same managers.
1927 Nov: Sold to Chenamskaya Azovskaya Kontora Sovtorgflot, Odessa, for £46,500. Odessa—Novosibirsk—Marseilles service. R/n *Dnepr*.
1933 Feb: Transferred to Vladivostok.
1941-5 Traded between Vladivostok area and Vancouver or Washington State ports.
1945 Aug: Was used as a supply ship at the relief of the Kurile Islands.
1958 No longer seagoing, *Dnepr* was towed to Nagovo Bay for use as a floating base for the Magadanskova Fish Trust.
1970 July: Converted by the addition of hull warehousing and accommodation superstructure into a base ship attached to the repair ship *Neva*.
1978 Broken up.

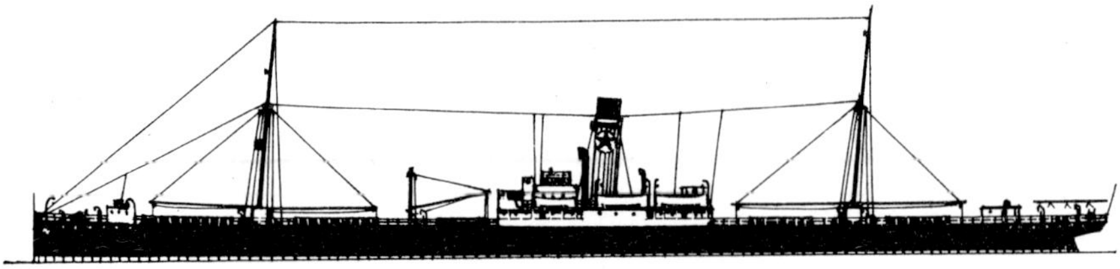

BRODHOLME/GOTHICSTAR/GOTHIC STAR (I)

10 **BRODHOLME/GOTHICSTAR/GOTHIC STAR (I)**
B 1899 Clydebank Eng. & Shipbuilding Co, Port Glasgow. **T** 5,673g, 3,628n.
D 420.5ft (128.17m) x 54.7 (16.67) x 28.8 (8.78).
E Sgl scr, tpl exp, 3 cyls, 493 NHP, 11 kts, 3 sgl ended blrs, Stm P: 160 lb. By builder.
H Steel. 2 dks. F 352 (107.29). P 50 (15.24). C 314,318 cu ft (6,900 cu ft) refrig. Crew 48.
1899 Feb: Delivered as *Nairnshire*, Elderslie S.S. Co, Turnbull Martin.
1910 Transferred to Scottish Shire Line.
1915 June: Acquired. r/n *Brodholme*, Brodholme S.S. Co.
1918 June 10: Torpedoed in the Mediterranean by *UC 53* but reached port.
1920 Union Cold Storage Co Ltd, became her owners with Blue Star (1920) Ltd managers. R/n *Gothicstar*.
1929 Name became *Gothic Star*.
1938 July 4: Arrived at Savona and scrapped. Realised £11,250.

BRODFIELD/BRODLEA/SAXONSTAR/SAXONSTAR (I)

11 **BRODFIELD**
B 1899 R. & W. Hawthorn Leslie & Co, Hebburn. **T** 5,455g, 3,498n.
D 420.4ft (128.14m) x 54ft (16.46m) x 28.6ft (8.72m).
E Sgl scr, tpl exp, 3 cyls, 505 NHP, 3 sgl ended blrs. Stm P: 160 lb, 11 kts. By builder.
H Steel. 2 dks. F 352ft (107.29m). P 50ft (15.24m). Flush decked in appearance.
1899 Sept: Delivered to Federal S.N. Co as *Surrey*.
1901 Engaged as a Boer War transport during the New Zealand—Cape Town leg of her inbound voyage.
1915 Feb 25: Struck a mine off Dunkirk. Beached at the North Downs near Deal and then towed into Dover. From there she was taken to the Thames Estuary and again beached before being unloaded at Tilbury. After repairs were effected she was purchased by Blue Star and renamed *Brodfield*, Brodfield S.S. Co.
1916 Nov 13: Wrecked near Church Point, Scilly Isles. The crew of 70 were all saved.

12 **BRODLEA/SAXONSTAR/SAXON STAR (I)**
Details as *Brodfield* (II) except: **T** 5,455g, 3,498n.
1899 March 11: Launched. June: Completed as *Kent* for the Federal S.N. Co.
1900 Carried New Zealand troops to the Boer War on her second inbound leg.
1915 Oct: Acquired by Blue Star Line Ltd and renamed *Brodlea*, Brodlea S.S. Co.
1920 Apr: Renamed *Saxonstar*, owned by Union Cold Storage Co with Blue Star (1920) Ltd as managers.

1929 Apr: The name became *Saxon Star* (I); owned by Blue Star Ltd.
1933 Laid up, River Tyne.
1934 Sept 17: Arrived at Savona for scrapping by S. A. Ricuperi Metallici after lay-up since January.

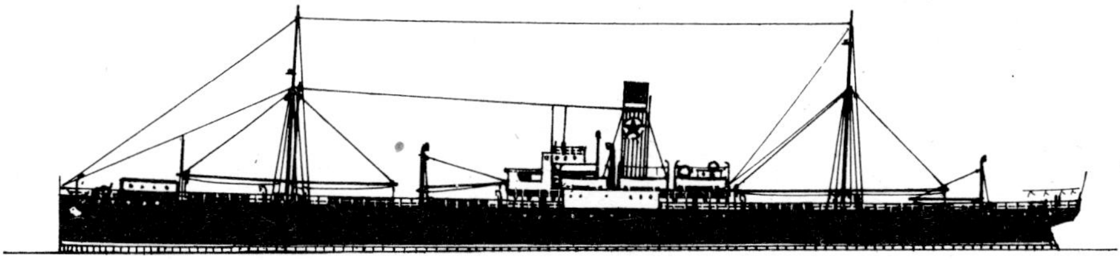

BRODMEAD/ROMANSTAR/ROMAN STAR (I)

13 **BRODMEAD/ROMANSTAR/ROMAN STAR (I)**
B 1895 R. & W. Hawthorn Leslie & Co, Hebburn. **T** 5,628g, 3,660n.
D 420ft (128.14m) x 54 (16.46) x 28.7 (8.75).
E Sgl scr, tpl exp, 3 cyls, 505 NHP, 3 sgl ended blrs, Stm P: 160 lb 11 kts. By builder.
H Steel. 2 dks. F 49 (14.93). B 266 (81.08). P 46 (14.02).
C 323,700 cu ft (9,166.2 cu m) refrig. Flush decked profile.
1895 Apr 25: Launched as *Rakaia* for the New Zealand Shipping Co. As built she had accommodation for 26 1st class and 250 'tween deck emigrant passengers.
1909 June: entered service. Carried the first load of frozen meat from Nelson, N.Z., to Britain.
1915 Feb: Became Blue Star Line's *Brodmead*, Brodmead S.S. Co.
1917 Sept 9: Torpedoed and then shelled in the Mediterranean by *UB-49*, her master Captain D. MacQueen being killed on the bridge. The ship escaped safely to Gibraltar.
1920 Apr: Renamed *Romanstar*, operated by Blue Star but registered under the name of Union Cold Storage.
1925 Aug 20: Loaded the first cargo of South African fruit for the U.K.
1929 May: Her name became *Roman Star*, owned by Blue Star Line Ltd.
1933 Laid up River Tyne for much of the time until sold.
1934 Sept 29: Only days after *Saxon Star* arrived at Savona *Roman Star* arrived at the scrap yard with *Tudor Star* virtually in her wake. The three ships had been sold to S. A. Ricuperi Metallici for £23,750.

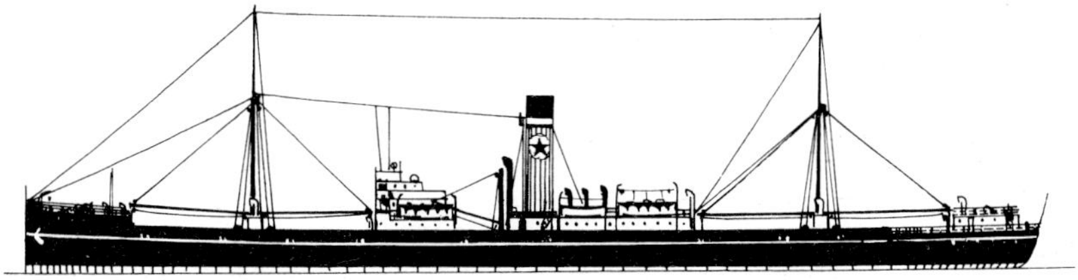

MONTILLA/GAELICSTAR/GAELIC STAR,
RUBIERA/IONICSTAR/IONIC STAR (I),
CAMANA/CELTICSTAR/CELTIC STAR (I)

14 **MONTILLA/GAELICSTAR/GAELIC STAR**
B 1917 Russell & Co, Port Glasgow. **T** 5,595g, 3,528n.
D 389.8ft (118.81m) x 53.2 (16.21) x 24.7 (7.53).
E Sgl scr, tpl exp, 3 cyls 548 NHP, 3 sgl ended blrs, Stm P: 200 lb 12 kts.
By D. Rowan & Co, Glasgow.

H Steel. 2 dks + shelter dk. F 50 (15.24). C 290,000 cu ft (8211.9 cu m) refrigerated in 20 chambers.
P 12.
1917 Feb 22: Launched as *Montilla* for the Montilla S.S. Co at a cost of £100,000. Managed by Blue Star Line. Aug: Completed.
1920 May: Renamed *Gaelicstar*; owned by Union Cold Storage.
1929 Apr: Became *Gaelic Star* with the owners now being Blue Star Line Ltd.
1949 Aug: Sold to Cia Genovese di Nav. a Vapori S.A., Genoa and renamed *Capo Noli*.
1950 Sold to Gestione Escercizio Navi, Genoa; same name.
1959 Jan: Broken up at Trieste by Sidemar.

15 RUBIERA/IONICSTAR/IONIC STAR (I)
Sister to *Montilla* (14) except: **T** 5,602g.
1917 June 28: Launched. Delivered as *Rubiera* for the Rubiera S.S. Co with Blue Star Line as managers.
1920 May: With the reorganisation of the company she was renamed *Ionicstar*; Blue Star Line (1920) Ltd as owners.
1929 Became *Ionic Star*.
1939 Oct 17: Went aground on the Crosby shore of the Mersey estuary one mile west of Formby Point and broke in two to become a total loss. Inbound from Brazil with cotton.

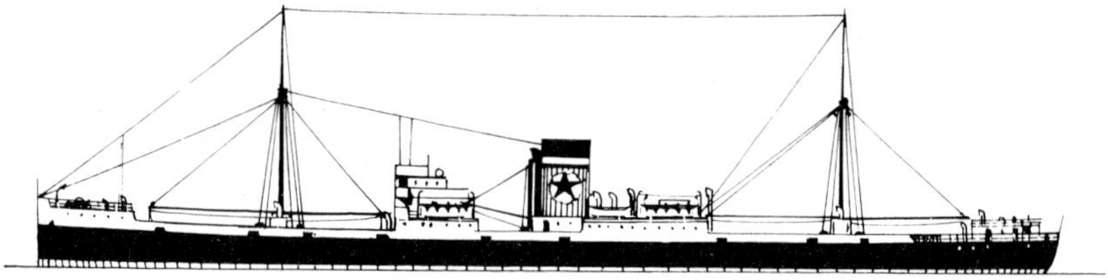

16A CELTIC STAR

16 **CAMANA/CELTICSTAR/CELTIC STAR (I)**
Sister to *Montilla* (14) except: **B** 1918 Dunlop, Bremner & Co, Port Glasgow.
T 5,575g. **D** 390.7ft (119.08m).
1917 Dec 3: Launched.
1918 June: Completed as *Camana*, Camana S.S. Co, with Blue Star Line as managers.
1920 Apr: Name became *Celticstar* with the Union Cold Storage as owners.
1929 Restyled *Celtic Star*.
1934 Nov 18: When she passed under Tower Bridge to berth at New Fresh Wharf in the Pool of London *Celtic Star* became the largest vessel so to do; although H.M.S. *Belfast* now holds that distinction. (See *Andalucia Star* (136)).
1935 The original tall and slender funnel was replaced by a shorter and fatter version which is alleged to have come from *Avelona Star*. (Drawing 16A.)
1939 Oct 18: Damaged in convoy by collision off the Cape Verde Islands.
1943 March 28: *Celtic Star* left Freetown independently for the U.K. and followed a zig-zag course. Next day, when 360 miles out, at 10.10pm the Italian submarine *Finzi* torpedoed her in No 2 hold, starboard side and the ship immediately commenced to sink. Boats 3 and 4 had been wrecked but numbers 1 and 2 pulled away safely. The vessel sank so quickly that those on board—some 25 men—had to jump for it. In 30 further seconds the ship had gone with the loss of only 2 lives. H.M.S. *Wastwater* picked up the survivors, 64 in all. Many of the men who jumped owed their lives to the fact that the ship still had way on her when she dived under; instead of being sucked down they were left behind. The Italians took one man prisoner, as proof of sinking, and gave cigarettes and matches to those in the boats.

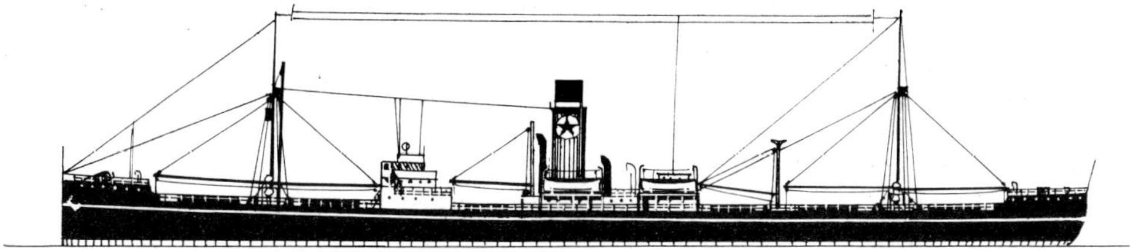

ROYALSTAR/ROYAL STAR (I), ALBIONSTAR/ALBION STAR (I), FRESNO STAR (I), TACOMA STAR (I), PACIFIC STAR (I)

17 **ROYALSTAR/ROYAL STAR (I)**
B 1919 Workman Clark & Co, Belfast. **T** 7,918g, 4,910n.
D 465ft (141.73) oa, 450 (137.16) x 58.5. (17.83) x 37.1 (11.31).
E Tw scr tpl exp, 2x3 cyls. 1,138 NHP, 3 dbl ended blrs, Stm P: 200 lb. 12 kts. By builder.
H Steel. 2 dks + shelter dk. F 43 (13.11). P 31 (9.44). C 368,590 cu ft (10,437.36 cu m) refrig.
1918 Nov 22: Launched as *War Charon* for the Shipping Controller. Standard 'G' type.
1919 Jan 24: Trials. Completed as *Royalstar*, Royalstar S.S. Co. Blue Star Line as managers. Feb: Entered service.
1920 May: Transferred to Union Cold Storage Ltd without change of name or operation.
1926 Nov: Gashed her hull open on an unchartered rock in the Malacca Strait. Made Singapore down by the head and docked stern first.
1929 Renamed *Royal Star*.
1934 The ship was bunkered with incorrect fuel which solidified in the double bottom. Placed in drydock at Smith's Dockyard, South Shields, a maze of steam pipes were fitted around and under the hull and then some 7 feet of water let in and steam heated until the fuel became viscous enough to be pumped out. A costly error.
1941 Mar 11: Damaged by bombs and machine gun fire off Stonehaven, Scotland.
1944 Apr 20: Damaged by torpedo bombers north east of Algiers enroute Buenos Aires—Algiers—Malta. On April 21 at 7.30am the Admiralty tug *Athlete*, from Algiers, took her in tow at 2 knots but the ship continued to settle and sank vertically at 11.7am to become the Company's final war loss.

18 **ALBIONSTAR/ALBION STAR (I)**
Details as *Royal Star* (17) except: **T** 7,920g, 4,908n.
1919 Mar 6: Launched as *War Hecuba* for the Shipping Controller, one of the Standard 'G' class. June 11: Trials and then handed over as *Albionstar*, Albionstar S.S. Co with Blue Star as managers. June: Maiden voyage to China and Japan.
1920 May: Transferred to Union Cold Storage; same name.
1929 Became *Albion Star*.
1930-32 Laid up.
1940 The space between the bridge and the funnel was filled with a deck house; 1 door, no portholes.
1948 Apr 23: Arrived at Briton Ferry, South Wales and broken up by Thos. W. Ward.

19 **FRESNO STAR (I)**
Details as *Royal Star* (17) except: **B** Barclay Curle & Co, Whiteinch. **T** 7,948g. **E** By builder. C 378,000 cu ft (10,703.8 cu m) bale or 430,000 cu ft (12,176.3 cu m) refrig. in 17 chambers.
1919 July 12: Launched. Laid down as *War Apollo* for the Shipping Controller. Standard 'G' type. Nov 26: Trials. Became *Woodarra*, British India S.N. Co. Ident: House and boats at mainmast.
1929 Aug: Acquired by Blue Star Line Ltd; renamed *Fresno Star*. Employed, as the name suggests, on the Pacific coast of North America route. Cost £60,000.
1933 Ownership was transferred to Union Cold Storage Co Ltd.
1935 Frederick Leyland & Co became the registered owners.

Aug: See *Napier Star* (33) entry.
1947 July 14: Arrived at Inverkeithing to be broken up by Thos. W. Ward.

20 **TACOMA STAR (I)**
Details as *Royal Star* (17) except: **T** 7,924g.
1919 April 30: Launched. Laid down as *War Theseus* for the Shipping Controller. Standard 'G' type. July 7: Trials. Completed as *Wangaretta* for British India S.N. Co. As in *Woodarra* (19) a deck house and lifeboat was fitted either side of the mainmast.
1929 Aug: Purchased with her sister ship by Blue Star; renamed *Tacoma Star* for service to the North Pacific west coast ports. Cost £60,000.
1933 Moved to Union Cold Storage ownership.
1935 Transferred to Frederick Leyland & Co.
1941 May 4: Sank in dock at Liverpool as a result of air raid bomb damage.
1942 Feb 1: 03.30 Torpedoed by *U-109* 380 miles short of Hampton Roads were she was to have joined a U.K. bound convoy. Apart from a distress signal no other trace of the ship was ever found. 94 lives were lost, including 9 gunners.

21 **PACIFIC STAR (I)**
Details as *Royal Star* (17) except: **B** Barclay Curle & Co, Whiteinch, Glasgow.
T 7,951g, 4,954n. **D** 449.1 ft (136.89m) bp x 58.2 (17.74).
E By builder with 2 dbl and 3 sgl ended blrs.
1919 Oct 29: Launched as *War Jupiter*, Shipping Controller, as one of the 29 Standard 'G' type of which only *War Icarus* had been completed at the time of the Armistice. Entered service as *Otaki* for the New Zealand Shipping Co.
1920 Feb 4: Maiden voyage Glasgow—Panama Canal—New Zealand.
1934 May 31: Sold to the Clan Line, Cayzer Irvine & Co, and renamed *Clan Robertson*.
1935 Sold to J. A. Billmeir's Stanhope Shipping Co (today a part of P. & O.'s former Townsend Thoresen Group) and renamed *Stanfleet*.
1939 Acquired by Zubi S.S. Co Ltd; became *Pacific Star*. Passed for £65,000 during the same year to Blue Star ownership without change of name.
1942 Oct 18: Inbound from Buenos Aires; sailed from Freetown in a fast 40 ship convoy destined for the Clyde. Oct 27: A submarine warning caused the convoy to zig-zag but *Pacific Star* was struck forward by a torpedo from *U-509* which reduced her speed so that she fell behind and made for Gibraltar but as the weather worsened course was set for the Canary Islands being then the nearest landfall. After forty-eight hours the vessel commenced to settle and Captain Evans was obliged to order 'Abandon ship' and 97 took to the boats. *Pacific Star* was last seen wallowing dead in the water with seas washing over her from stem to stern. Incidentally *U-509* torpedoed Blue Funnel's *Stentor* five minutes after *Pacific Star*.

EMPIRESTAR/EMPIRE STAR (I)/TUDOR STAR (II)

22 **EMPIRESTAR/EMPIRE STAR (I)/TUDOR STAR (II)**
B 1919 Lithgows, Port Glasgow. **T** 7,199g, 4,524n.
D 423.4 ft (129.05m) x 56 (17.07) x 28.7 (8.75).

E Sgl scr, tpl exp, 3 cyls, 696 NHP, 4 sgl ended blrs, Stm P: 200 lb; 12 kts.
By J. G. Kincaid & Co, Greenock.
H Steel. 2 dks and shelter dk. C 388,000 cu ft (10,987 cu m) refrig.
1919 Dec: Completed as *Empirestar*, owned by Empirestar S.S. Co, with Blue Star Line as managers. Entered service with an Admiralty cowl topped funnel. The vessel had open deck under the bridge deck superstructure on the starboard side but port was as drawn.
1920 Oct: Transferred to Union Cold Storage ownership; managers unchanged.
1927 Oct 25: Aided in the rescue of the passengers and crew of the Italian *Principessa Mafalda* (Nav. Gen. Italiana) 200 miles off the coast of Brazil. The ship was sinking in calm seas after the loss of a propeller shaft had caused unstoppable flooding; 303 lives lost.
1929 Renamed *Empire Star*, Blue Star Line as owners. The cowl top of the funnel was removed at this time.
1935 To make way for the advent of *Empire Star* (II) the vessel was renamed *Tudor Star* (II).
1949 Transferred to the ownership of Union International Co Ltd.
1950 Broken up at Hendrik-ido-Ambacht, Netherlands. Price £20,000.

MAGICSTAR

23 **MAGICSTAR**
B 1893 R. & W. Hawthorn Leslie, Hebburn-on-Tyne. **T** 5,534g, 3,403n.
D 420 ft (128.02m) x 54 (16.46) x 28.7 (8.75).
E Sgl scr, tple exp, 3 cyls, 534 NHP, 11 kts; 2 sgl ended blrs, Stm P: 160 lb. By builder.
H Steel. 2 dks + shelter dk. F 49 (14.93). B 262 (79.86). P 41 (8.75).
C 315,234 cu ft (8,926.5 cu m) refrig.
P 25 1st
1893 Oct 10: Launched as *Buteshire* for Turnbull Martin's Elderslie S.S. Co. Her sister ship being the *Perthshire*. Square rigged foremast.
1910 Ownership transferred to Scottish Shire Line.
1915 Became *Bollington Grange*, Houlder Bros and transferred from the Australian to the South American run. Pole masted.
1916 Transferred to Furness Houlder Argentine Lines and renamed *Canonesa*.
1918 May 1: Torpedoed by *UB-57* off Worthing and beached. Salvaged and repaired at Southampton.
1919 Purchased at Southampton and renamed *Magicstar* and owned by the Brodway S.S. Co with Blue Star Line as managers.
1920 Transferred to Union Cold Storage ownership. Shortly afterwards the well decks were plated over to give the ship a flush profile. The fcsl lighthouses were also replaced with two small store lockers with only 2 ports in each.
1929 Laid up pending sale for demolition and therefore not renamed *Magic Star*.
1930 Broken up by Thos. W. Ward at Inverkeithing, Firth of Forth.

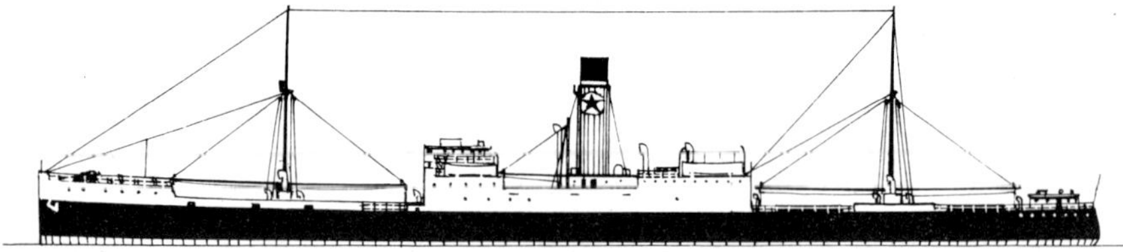

ALMEDA (I)/NORMANSTAR/NORMAN STAR (I)

24 **ALMEDA (I)/NORMANSTAR/NORMAN STAR (I)**

B 1919 Dunlop Bremner & Co, Port Glasgow. **T** 6,996g, 4,432n.
D 415.6 ft (126.76m) x 56.2 (17.13) x 25.5 (7.77).
E Sgl scr, tpl exp, 3 cyls, 662 NHP, 12 kts. Stm P: 200 lb, 3 sgl ended blrs. By builder.
H Steel. 2 dks + awning dk. F 56 (17.06). B 130 (39.62).
C 347,408 cu ft (9,837.5 cu m) refrig.

1919 Apr 19: Launched as *Almeda* for Almeda S.S. Co, Blue Star Line as managers. Oct: completed as *Normanstar* for Normanstar S.S. Co. This ship had no sister ships and was really a product of wartime design and building.
1920 Transferred to Union Cold Storage ownership.
1929 Renamed *Norman Star* (I).
1941 Jan 16: Bombed at Avonmouth. Fires put out.
1949 Transferred to Union International Co.
1950 Mar 7: Arrived at Blyth, Northumberland for scrapping by Hughes Bolckow.

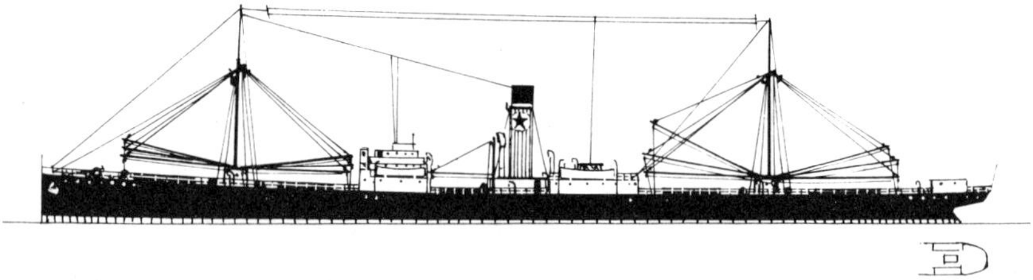

LUSIADA/VIKINGSTAR/VIKING STAR

25 **LUSIADA/VIKINGSTAR/VIKING STAR**

B 1920 Napier & Miller & Co, Glasgow. **T** 6,445g, 3,928n.
D 400.3 ft (122.01m) x 52.3 (15.94) x 28.5 (8.69).
E Sgl scr, tpl exp, 3 cyls, 517 NHP, 10 kts; Stm P: 180 lb, 3 sgl ended blrs.
By Dunsmuir & Jackson, Glasgow.
H Steel. 2 dks + shelter dk. Flush. C 323,697 cu ft (9,166.13 cu m) refrig.

1919 Nov 28: Launched as *Lusiada*, Lusiada S.S. Co, Brazil. Blue Star as managers. Cowl top funnel.
1920 Feb: Completed as *Vikingstar* for Blue Star Line (1920) Ltd, London.
1929 Renamed *Viking Star*.
1942 Aug 25: 4.50pm, 26 days out from Buenos Aires for the U.K. the ship was 180 miles off Freetown, under the command of Captain Mills, when she was struck by two torpedoes from *U-130* which broke her in two, sinking her within minutes. The sole lifeboat, with 36 aboard, reached land on August 29 and two liferafts, after a horrific ordeal at sea, were washed ashore on September 4 on the coast of Liberia with 12 more survivors. In all only 8 lives were lost.

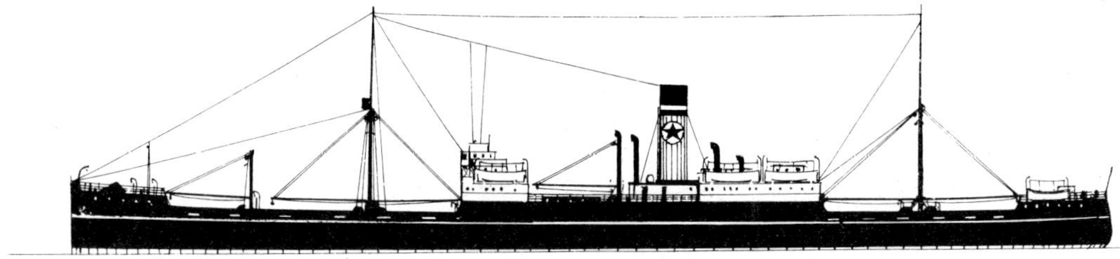

A. DORICSTAR/DORIC STAR

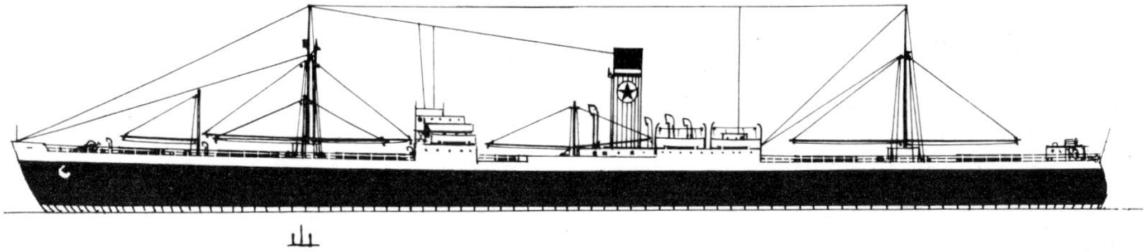

B. DORIC STAR

26 **DORICSTAR/DORIC STAR**
B 1921 Lithgows Port Glasgow. **T** 10,441g, 8,503n.
D 499.8 (152.34) x 64 (19.5) x 37 (11.28).
E Sgl scr, 2 dbl reduction geared turbines, 1,398 NHP, 6 sgl ended blrs, Stm P: 200 lb. 14 kts. By Metropolitan Vickers Electric Co, Manchester.
H Steel. 3 dks + shelter dk. F 44 (13.41). B 192 (58.52). P 47 (14.32).
C 461,000 cu ft (13,054.1 cu m) refrig. in 18 chambers.
1921 Feb 24: Launched as *Doricstar* and owned by Eastmans Ltd, the retail meat shop chain owned by Vestey's ; managed by Blue Star Line. Oct: The vessel commenced her career on the China run bringing frozen pork to the U.K.
1929 Renamed *Doric Star*. (Drawing 26A).
1933-4 Lengthened to 529.8 ft (161.48m) at Jarrow by the fitting of a new fore part and a Maier bow. Speed 15 kts. Placed on the Australia route. (Drawing 26B).
1938 Owned by Union Cold Storage Ltd.
1939 Dec 2: Inbound. Sunk by gunfire and a final torpedo from the German pocket battleship *Admiral Graf Spee* in the South Atlantic 19.15S,05.05E. Her commander, Captain Stubbs, used wireless until stopped by gunfire. He was also able to convince the boarding party that the cargo was wool whereas this was only the uppermost layer. Food was the remainder. The crew of *Doric Star* became prisoners aboard the *Altmark* until rescued by H.M.S. *Cossack* in Norwegian waters. The captain was kept on board *Graf Spee* but was released at Montevideo prior to her self-destruction after the Battle of the River Plate.

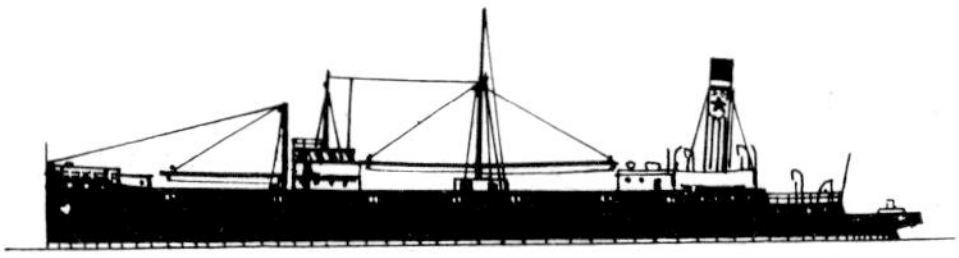

BRITANICA

27 **BRITANICA**
B 1913 Cammell Laird & Co, Birkenhead. **T** 1,350g, 774n.
D 220 (67.05) x 42.1 (12.83) x 9.9 (3.02).
E Tw scr, comp inv, 2x2 cyls each fired by one sgl ended blr. Stm P: 140 lb.
H Steel. 1 dk. F&B 208 (63.4). C Refrig. in 4 holds of 4 compartments each.
1913 Jan 22: Launched as *Doon* for Royal Mail S.P. Co; one of three feeder vessels based at Buenos Aires for River Plate service. Flew the Argentine flag.
1919 Used for Continent-U.K. feeder services (in conjunction with R.M.S.P. Co's *Eider*). Late in the year sold to Las Palmas Produce Co. Renamed *Britanica*.
1923 Sold to Anglo-South American Meat Co, Buenos Aires.
1924 Acquired by Union Cold Storage Co, Blue Star as managers; same name. Registered for use as a cargo distributor not beyond Brest or Hamburg.
1936 Owned by Blue Star Line.
1941 Nov: Became a store ship at Scapa Flow.
1946 Jan: Arrived at Singapore for use as a cold meat storeship.
1947 Oct: Left Singapore for London after six months laid up at anchor.
1948 Feb: Laid up at the Royal Victoria Dock, London, with defective engines. Sold to L. & J. Engelen, Boom, Belgium, and reduced to a barge for the carriage of scrap metal between Antwerp and Willebroek. No further history.

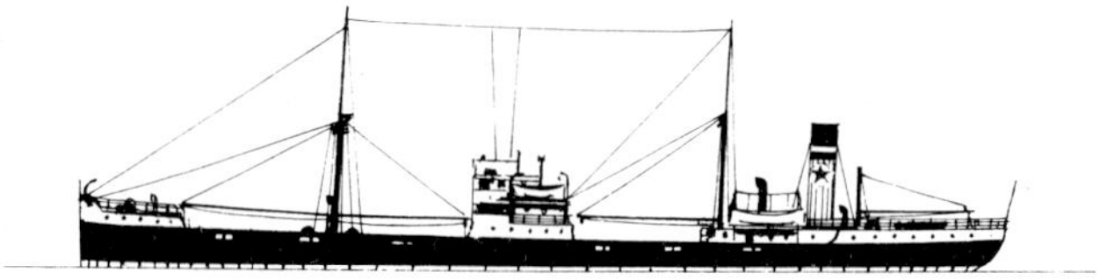

KAOLACK

28 **KAOLACK**
B 1917 Ateliers et Chantiers de la Loire, St. Nazaire. **T** 1,843g, 1,021n.
D 268.8 (81.93) x 35.8 (10.91) x 19.1 (5.82). **E** Tw scr.
H Steel. 2 dks. F 41 (12.5). B 39 (11.89). P 59 (17.98).
1916 June 15: Launched for De Chanaud & Cie, Paris.
1917 Jan: Completed for Soc. Coloniale d'Alimentation Frigorifique; same group.
1921 Owned by Cie Francaise du Froid; same name.
1924 Bought by Union Cold Storage for their China salt trade. Same name. Served Almeria—Shanghai—Kobe.
1925 Quarantined at Taku Bar with Cholera. One death.
1933 Laid up River Tyne.
1935 Sold to Crete Shipping Co, London. Stelp & Leighton managers.
1938 Spanish Civil War blockade runner; owned by Claude Angel & Co, Cardiff. Nov 25: Bomb damage at Valencia.
1939 Purchased by Zubi Shipping Co who also acquired *Pacific Star* (21).
1946 Sold to Empresa Nacional 'Elcano' de la Marine Merrcante; r/n *Artico*.
1949 Used as a fish factory storage ship by Industrias Pesquerias Africanas S.A. Spanish Morocco based.
1955 Reverted to 'Elcano'.
1957 Broken up by Metalurgica Navarra, Cadiz.

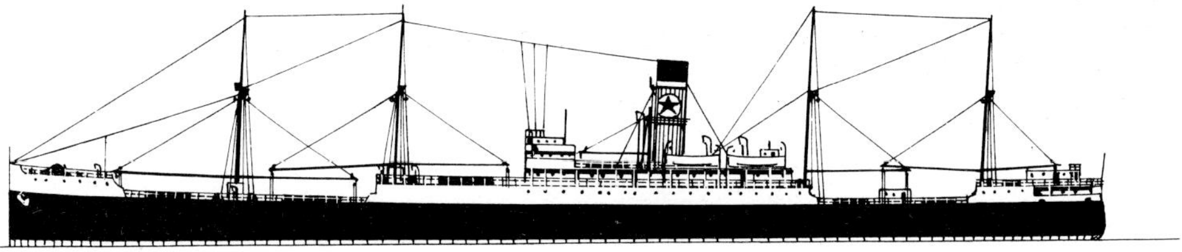

TROJANSTAR/TROJAN STAR (I)

29 **TROJANSTAR/TROJAN STAR (I)**
B 1916 Ateliers et Chantiers de France, Dunkirk. **T** 9,257g, 5,612n. 12,600 dwt.
D 473.8 (144.41) x 60 (18.29) x 36.6 (11.16).
E Tw scr, 2 x tpl exp, 3 cyls + dbl reduction geared turb with hydraulic coupling; 1,106 NHP, 5 sgl ended blrs, Stm P: 200 lb; 13 kts. By builder.
H Steel. 2 dks + shelter dk. F 48 (14.63). B 189 (57.61).
C 691,000 cu ft (19,567 cu m) g.
1916 Nov 9: Launched as *Aberdeenshire*, Scottish Shire Line, but taken over by the French Government and completed in 1920 as *La Perouse* for the French Line's subsidiary Soc. Gen. d'Armaments Maritimes, Le Havre. Ownership was, however, retained by the Government. Pass: 300.
1920 Made 2 voyages for French Line; laid up as uneconomical.
1923 Chartered to the Northern Steamship Co for service across the North Atlantic.
1924 Acquired by Union Cold Storage Co Ltd; renamed *Trojanstar*, Blue Star as Managers. Pass: 12. Refrigerated capacity installed.
1928 Oct: A steampipe burst which resulted in an engine room fire.
1929 Renamed *Trojan Star*.
1934 May: Enroute Auckland—London *Trojan Star* encountered fuel trouble and had to put back when 500 miles out. The oil in the double bottom tanks became so treacly that it could not be pumped. Later in this year she made the Company's first call at Avonmouth.
1935 The ship was renovated at North Shields by Smith's Dockyard for the Australian service. To increase her operating speed her machinery was improved by adding 2 Bauer Wach exhaust steam turbines to each screw and superheaters to the boilers. Oil fuel. The effect was to increase the speed by 2 knots. Larger bunkers also had to be installed. She emerged from the refit without her main and mizzen topmasts.
1954 Aug 27: Sailed from Newport, Monmouthshire, on her final voyage. It was to be long and arduous. A serious fire off Columbo, a leaking stern gland, weather damage and even an engine breakdown occurred before her return to London in April 1955.
1955 May 25: Arrived at Blyth for breaking up by Hughes Bolckow of the British Iron & Steel Corporation; by then very much the veteran of the fleet.

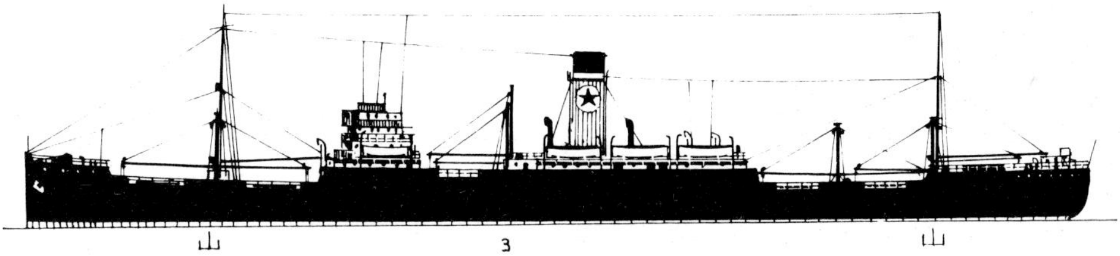

A. STUARTSTAR (II)/STUART STAR, AFRICSTAR/AFRIC STAR (I), RODNEYSTAR/RODNEY STAR, RALEIGHSTAR/NAPIERSTAR/NAPIER STAR

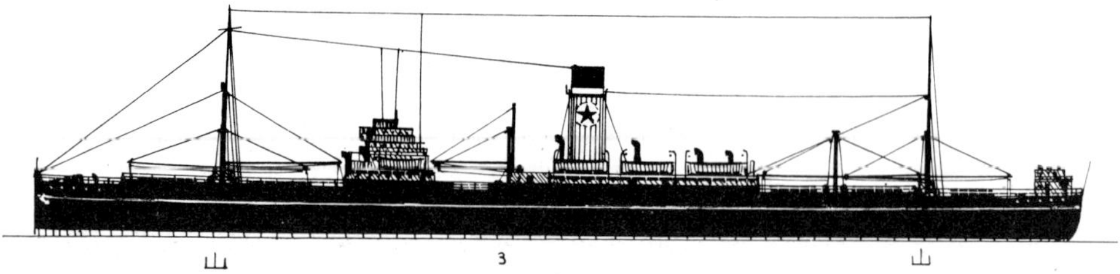

3

B. STUART STAR, AFRIC STAR (I)

30 **STUARTSTAR (II)/STUART STAR**
B 1926 Palmer's Co, Newcastle. **T** 11,884g, 7,430n.
D 475.8 (145.02) x 67.3 (20.51) x 45.2 (13.78).
E Tw scr, 2 x 2 sgl reduction geared turbs, 1,582 NHP, 4 blrs 200 psi. 14 kts.
By Parson's Marine Steam Turbine Co, Newcastle.
H Steel. 4 + part 5th dks. F 39 (11.88). B 200 (60.96). P 72 (21.94).
C 540,000 cu ft (15,291.2 cu m), 511,000 cu ft (14.470 cu m) refrig. in 55 chambers.
1926 Mar 15: Launched as *Stuartstar*, one of four sisters built in pairs at two yards. Cost £210,000 each without refrigeration which was installed by outside contractors. Oct: Entered service.
1928 July: An experimental pulverised coal burning boiler was installed to replace the oil burner. Being successful the ship was fully converted.
1929 May: R/n *Stuart Star*.
1935 The ship was rebuilt by decking over the wells to give a flush profile. (Drawing 30B).
1937 Nov 20: Departed Liverpool for Australia via Cape Town and Lourenco Marques. Dec 17: At 10.00, in thick fog, the ship was wrecked at Hood Point Light, near to East London. The stern broke off in the swell and she became a total loss.

31 RODNEYSTAR/RODNEY STAR
Details as *Stuartstar* (30) except: **B** Lithgows, Port Glasgow. **T** 11,803g, 7,416n.
D 476ft (145.08m). **E** By builder.
1926 Apr 14: Launched as *Rodneystar*.
1927 Jan: Delivered.
1929 Renamed *Rodney Star*.
1935 Rebuilt similarly to *Stuartstar* except for full deck houses.
1941 May 16: 420 miles off Freetown torpedoed three times in the early hours by *U-105* during a tropical rain storm when enroute from Buenos Aires for Liverpool. The ship broke in two but remained afloat. The survivors in the lifeboats were inadvertently shelled when the U-boat wastefully loosed off 78 shells in order to aid the doomed vessel's demise. The crew were picked up 6 days later by a destroyer and taken to Takoradi. A further group had covered 298 miles before being picked up by the French and taken to Dakar where they were exchanged for a French crew that were in British hands.

31 **AFRICSTAR/AFRIC STAR (I)**
Details as *Stuartstar* (30) except: **T** 11,867g, 7,425n.
1926 May 11: Launched. Nov: Completed as *Africstar*. Refrigeration plant fitted after handing over.
1929 Renamed *Afric Star*.
1941 Jan 29: Sunk by the German raider *Kormoran* enroute Buenos Aires—Trinidad—London position 08N25W. *Kormoran* was disguised as a Russian until breaking out her ensign prior to the attack. The survivors were later taken to Bordeaux, and internment, by the Hapag freighter *Portland*.

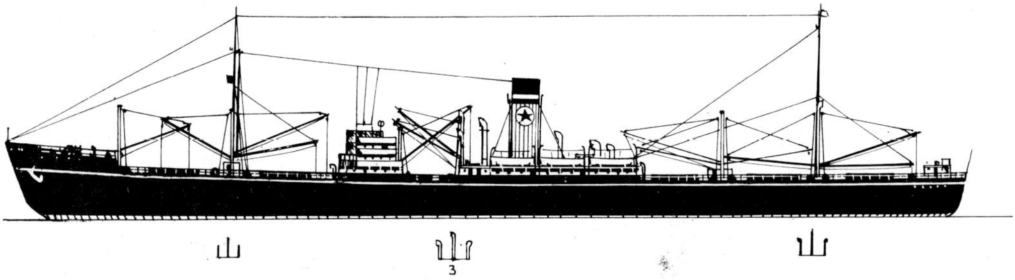

A. NAPIER STAR (I) as rebuilt

33 **RALEIGHSTAR/NAPIERSTAR/NAPIER STAR (I)**
Details as *Stuartstar* (30) except: **B** Lithgows, Port Glasgow. **T** 10,583, 6,527n. **E** By builder. **D** 476ft (145.08m).
1926 Aug 5: Launched as *Raleighstar*.
1927 March: Entered service as *Napierstar*. Identification: Her funnel and poop derrick posts were cowelled not capped. Clearly intended to trade to New Zealand because of her name.
1929 R/n *Napier Star*.
1935 Aug 18: Enroute Glasgow—Liverpool to complete loading for New Zealand. *Napier Star* came into head on collision with White Star's *Laurentic* 40 miles out from the Mersey Bar lightship. *Laurentic* was outward bound on one of her seven day cruises to the Northern Capitals of Europe. Both vessels were badly damaged forward but *Laurentic* was able to take *Napier Star* in tow until the arrival of the salvage tugs. Preliminary repairs were carried out at Liverpool while her cargo was off-loaded into *Fresno Star* who took the sailing manned by many of *Napier Star's* crew (those of *Fresno Star* being on homecoming leave). The damaged vessel then proceeded to the Tyne for permanent repairs.

Lengthened by 24ft (7.31m) and a Maier bow fitted. The wells fore and aft were plated over and a topgallent fcsle added to produce a powerful looking ship. Drawing 33A.
1940 Dec 18: 3.55pm, torpedoed by *U-100* (Schepke) and sunk in gale conditions 300 miles south west of Ireland outward bound for New Zealand with 17 passengers and a crew of 82. The Swedish freighter *Vaalaren* came upon one lifeboat which contained 2 women passengers and 12 crew. 84 had perished.

34 ALMEDA (II/ALMEDA STAR (I), ANDALUCIA/ANDALUCIA STAR (I), AVILA/AVILA STAR (I), AVELONA/AVELONA STAR (I), ARANDORA/ANDORA STAR

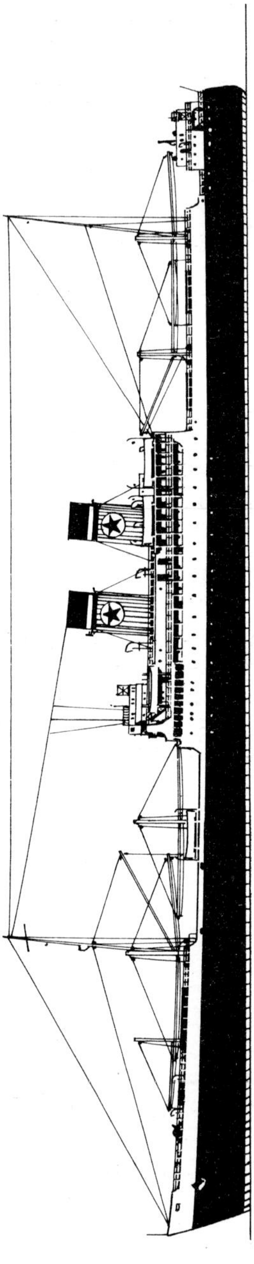

34A ALMEDA STAR (I), ANDALUCIA STAR (I), AVILA STAR (I)

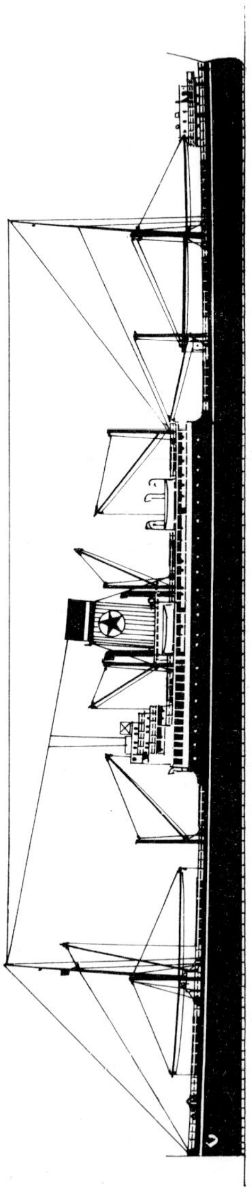

37A AVELONA STAR (I)

34 **ALMEDA (II)/ALMEDA STAR (I)**
B 1926 Cammell Laird & Co, Birkenhead. **T** 12,838g, 7,826n, 9,400 dwt.
D 535 (163.1) oa, 512.2 (156.1) x 68.3 (20.82) x 43 (10.36). Dft 27.5 (8.38).
E Tw scr, 2 x 2 Parson's 22,000 rpm turbs (1 HP + 1 LP with astern incorporated in LP), sgl reduction geared to 120 rpm. 8,000 IHP, 3 dbl + 2 sgl Howden blrs. 200 psi. 17 kts. By builder. After funnel dummy.
H Steel. 3 + part 4th dks. F 78 (23.77). B 285 (86.86). P 68 (20.72). Prom dk 170 (51.82). 6 hatches. C 419,980 cu ft (11,878 cu m) refrig. 27 x 3 ton derricks. 1 x 110 ton to foremast.
P 180 1st in superior accommodation.
1926 June 29: Launched as *Almeda*, the first of three from the builder at a cost of £910,000 the trio.
1927 Feb 16: Inaugurated Blue Star Line's London—South America passenger service.
1929 Renamed *Almeda Star*.
1935 Lengthened by 65.7 ft (20.02m) and a Maier bow fitted. Pass: 150 1st. T 14,935. (Drawing 34A).
1937 May 28: Went aground in fog outside Boulogne enroute for Tilbury. Refloated the next day.
1937 The mainmast was removed.
1940 Dec 22: Damaged by bombs during an air raid on Liverpool.
1941 Jan 17: 07.45 Sunk by torpedo from *U-86* 250 miles west of the Outer Hebrides. There was a full gale blowing at the time and all 194 passengers and 166 crew were lost without trace.

35 **ANDALUCIA/ANDALUCIA STAR (I)**
Details as *Almeda* (34) except: **B** 1927 **T** 12,846g, 7,830n.
1926 Sept 21: Launched as *Andalucia* for the South American passenger service.
1927 Mar: Entered service.
1929 May: R/n *Andalucia Star*. Ident: No faring forward of the bridge.
1935 Lengthened and refitted similarly to *Almeda Star*. T 14,934g.
1937 Mainmast removed.
1942 Oct 7: 21.00: Struck by two torpedoes from *U-107* in numbers 5 and 6 holds when 200 miles west of Freetown enroute Buenos Aires—U.K. 78 passengers out of 83 and all but two of the crew were picked by by H.M.S. *Petunia*. Oct 8: The survivors arrived at Freetown and were transferred for passage to England to *President Doumer*, Messageries Maritimes. The loss of *Almeda Star* meant that all five of the 'A' class passenger liners had now been sunk.

36A ARANDORA STAR

36B ARANDORA STAR

36 **ARANDORA/ARANDORA STAR**

Details as *Almeda* (34) except: **B** 1927 **T** 12,838g, 7,818n, 9,402 dwt.
E 8,400 SHP at 120 rpm. **H** 2 dks part 4-8 C 415,000 cu ft (11,751 cu m) refrig. in 49 chambers. A lift was also included. **P** 162 1st.
1927 Jan 14: Launched. May 29: Entered service. She was actually the last of the five but the third of the Cammell Laird trio.
1929 Converted into a cruise liner at Fairfield S.B. & E. Co. Emerged as *Arandora Star*. June 15: First sailing Immingham—Norway. Thereafter based at Southampton. Pass: 400. Equipped with swimming pool, ballroom and a parade of shops. The conversion cost £210,000 (Drawing 36A).
1931 White hull, red band.
1935 Further modifications took place. Blue banded hull. (Drawing 36B).
1938 Overhauled at Southampton. Vent-Axia ventilation installed in the public rooms and main cabins.
1939 Sept 3: On her 125th cruise, bound for New York, she was recalled to Southampton following the outbreak of war. Sept 29: Laid up at Falmouth. Dec 21: Used at Avonmouth as a test ship for net defences against torpedo attack. Later converted into a troopship.
1940 June 4: Evacuated 1,600 men from Narvik to Glasgow. Then proceeded to Brest and Quiberon Bay and brought troops back to England. *Arandora Star* then returned to Bayonne where she again evacuated troops; this time she was under constant bomb attack and was obliged to keep moving while the men came out in boats. Returning once more to France she now embarked 1,700 persons from St. Jean de Luz arriving back in Liverpool on June 29 after an extraordinarily outstanding month's work.
June 30: Embarked German and Italian internees for transfer to St. Johns, Newfoundland.
July 2: Left Liverpool with 479 German and 734 Italian male internees plus 86 German prisoners of war guarded by 200 troops and with a crew of 174.
June 3: 6.15am, torpedoed by *U-47* 75 miles west of Bloody Foreland. The ship sank in 65 minutes. At noon the Canadian destroyer *St. Laurent* arrived and in 5 hours picked out of the water 868 persons. 805 lives were lost; it is said that many more might have been saved had not the Italians resolutely refused to leave the sinking ship until it actually sank. 55 of *Arandora Star's* crew and 37 military were among the missing.

37 **AVELONA/AVELONA STAR (I)**

Details as *Almeda* (34) except: **B** 1927 John Brown & Co, Clydebank.
T 13,376g **E** By builder with Parsons equipment.
H F 80 (24.38). B 245 (74.68). P 85 (25.91). C 425,000 cu ft (12,034.7 cu m)
P 162 1st-de-Luxe.
1926 Dec 6: Launched. Cost £305,000.
1927 May: Trials. As built had Admiralty topped funnels.
May 20: Maiden voyage London—Madeira—Rio de Janeiro—Santos—Montevideo—Buenos Aires.
1928 All the 'A's with Admiralty tops had them removed.
1929 May: Renamed *Avelona Star*.

1931 Due to passenger overcapacity aggravated by the growing depression in world trade the ship was converted at Greenock into a cargo ship. Apart from closing in the well decks the passenger accommodation was removed and the dummy after funnel discontinued. Surprisingly the bridge superstructure was moved bodily forward by some 8ft (2.44m) to give a vertical profile. C 647,000 cu ft (18,321 cu m) refrig. in 80 chambers.
1934 The ship was modified into its final form (Drawing 37A). C 651,699 cu ft (18,454m) refrig; the largest capacity in any vessel then afloat.
1939 Aug 4: The ship was at Dakar when war was declared and went straight to Buenos Aires to load meat.
1940 May: Left Buenos Aires for Freetown; there, on June 15, she joined a convoy for the U.K. Next day, in company with 33 others, *Avelona Star* sailed.
June 30: 9.30pm, torpedoed by *U-43* 200 miles off Cape Finisterre and sank the following day. The 80 survivors were picked up by the French steamer *Beignon*, which in doing so fell behind the convoy and was herself torpedoed by *U-30*. The joint survivors in the sea, 120 men, were taken from the water by the escorting destroyers *Vesper* and *Windsor*. Despite all of this only 4 of *Avelona Star's* crew were lost.

38 **AVILA/AVILA STAR (I)**
Details as *Almeda* (34) except: **B** 1927 John Brown & Co, Clydebank.
T 12,872g, 7,878n. **D** As *Avelona* **P** 162.
1926 Sept 22: Launched as *Avila*, Admiralty tops to funnels.
1927 March: Delivered.
1928 Funnels uncapped.
1929 May: Renamed *Avila Star*.
1934 Nov 25: Arrived at Swan, Hunter, Wallsend for lengthening by 39ft (11.9m) and the fitting of a Maier bow.
1935 Mar: Returned to service.
1942 July 6: 00.39. After leaving Buenos Aires, commanded by Captain Fisher and with 30 passengers and a crew of 166, the ship was torpedoed by *U-201* 90 miles west of Azores enroute for the U.K. A second torpedo struck underneath a lifeboat throwing the occupants into the sea. Her commander was the last to leave the doomed vessel and was drowned. Next day the five surviving lifeboats were separated in worsening weather; soon afterwards the Portuguese destroyer *Lima* picked up the 110 men from three of the boats and landed them at Punta Delgada in the Azores.
July 22: One of the remaining two boats was seen by an aircraft and the Portuguese sloop *Pedro Nunes* was directed to them. The fifth lifeboat was, unfortunately, never seen again. 73 lives were lost.

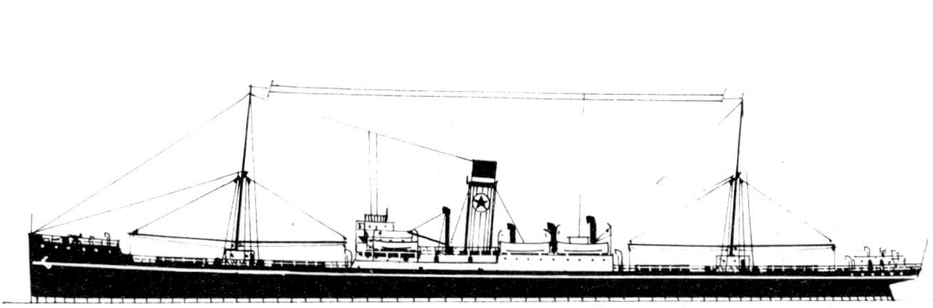

3

OREGONSTAR/OREGON STAR (I)

39 **OREGONSTAR/OREGON STAR (I)**
B 1914 Hawthorn Leslie & Co, Hebburn. **T** 5,714g, 3,620n.
D 426.3 (129.94) x 54.1 (16.49) x 29.3 (8.93).

E Sgl scr, quad exp, 4 cyls, 747 NHP, 4 sgl end blrs; Stm P: 220 lb; 12 kts. By N. E. Marine Eng Co, Newcastle.
H Steel 2 dks + shelter dk. F 50 (15.24). **P** 25.
1913 Ordered by William Milburn & Co, prior to the formation of Port Line.
1914 Feb 12: Launched. The first Board meeting of the Port Line (viz Commonwealth & Dominion Line), was not held until Feb 28.
May 29: Delivered to Port Line as *Port Albany*.
1929 Feb: Acquired for £40,000 by Union Cold Storage Co; r/n *Oregonstar*. May: R/n *Oregon Star*. P 12.
1932 Nov 13: Caught fire and burnt out at Palmer's yard, Hebburn, during a refit. Declared a total loss.
1933 At anchor in the River Tyne.
1934 Sold by the Underwriters for £5,350 to Hughes Bolckow. May 1: Arrived at Blyth for scrapping.

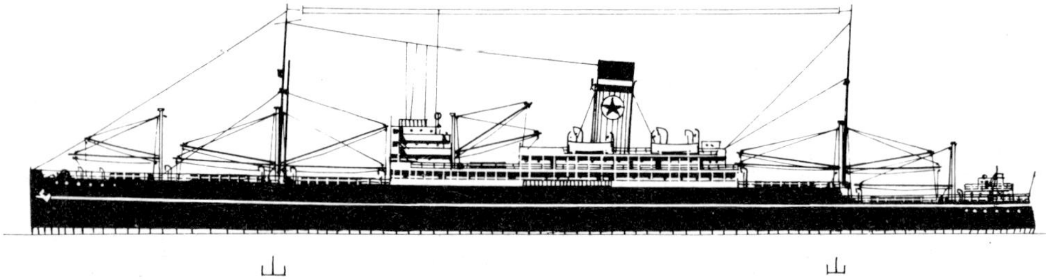

SULTAN STAR

40 **SULTAN STAR**
B 1930 Cammell Laird & Co, Birkenhead. **T** 12,306g, 7,684n.
D 486.1 (148.16) x 70.2 (6.52) x 36.4 (11.09).
E tw scr, 3 dbl reduction geared turb to each scr, 1,870 NHP, Stm P: 230, 14 kts. By builder.
H Steel. 3 dks + pt 4th; F&B 414 (126.19). C 626,000 cu ft (17.743 cu m) refrig. in 80 chambers.
P 12 1st. Crew 72.
1929 Oct 4: Launched for Blue Star Line Ltd.
1930 Feb: Inaugurated the service to New Zealand.
1933 Transferred to Union Cold Storage Co ownership. Dec: Made the Company's first call at Timaru, N.Z.
1935 Ownership became Frederick Leyland & Co. During the year rebuilding and modification took place.
1940 Feb 14: 16.30; torpedoed by *U-48* off Lands End. The ship had arrived in home waters in company of H.M.S. *Exeter* returning severely damaged from the Battle of the River Plate who in turn was being escorted by the battleship *Barham* and the destroyers *Vesper* and *Whitshed*. When the *Sultan Star* parted company the shadowing submarine followed and sank her. *Vesper* and *Whitshed* raced back to depth charge the U-boat before picking up the survivors. Blue Star records say that the U-boat was sunk but *U-48* was not actually sunk until May 3 1945 (in the Caribbean).

TUSCAN STAR (I)

41 **TUSCAN STAR (I)**
B 1930 Palmer's Co, Newcastle. **T** 11,449g, 7,075n.
D 471 (143.56) x 68.3 (20.82) x 35.1 (10.7).
E Tw scr, oil, 2 strke sgl acting 2 x 8 cyls 1,994 NHP 15 kts. By Sulzer Bros, Winterthur, installed by Palmer's.
H Steel 3 dks + pt 4th. F 71 (21.64). B 285 (86.87) C 566,700 cu ft (16,047.2 cu m) refrig. in 36 chambers.
1929 Oct 31: Launched; Blue Star Line's first motorship.
1930 Apr: Placed on the New Zealand service.
1933 Transferred to Union Cold Storage ownership.
1935 Registered in the name of Frederick Leyland & Co.
1939 Dec 17: Damaged by air attack in the English Channel. The bombs fell just wide but the ship was then machine gunned and hit by cannon fire.
1942 Sept 6: 23.50; torpedoed twice in quick succession by *U-109* 450 miles out from Freetown inbound from Santos. She sank in 15 minutes. Aboard were 26 passengers and 88 crew. 9 lives were lost in the explosion and the remainder took to the boats. When by searchlight, the submarine saw women and children in one lifeboat tinned food was passed over to them. Next day the Orient liner *Otranto* picked up that lifeboat; all the others reached land safely.

BRODSTONE (II)

42 **BRODSTONE (II)**
B 1934 Alexander Hall & Co, Aberdeen. **T** 72g 6n.
D 75.6 (23.04) x 18.1 (5.52) x 7.1 (2.16).
E Sgl scr, oil, 8 cyls 4 stroke, sgl acting, 122 NHP, 8 kts. By Mirrlees, Bickerton & Day, Manchester.
H Steel. 1 dk.
1934 Oct: Launched. A tug for use on the River Thames.
1935 Entered service owned by Frederick Leyland with Blue Star as managers. Union Cold Storage became operators and *Brodstone* wore their funnel markings which were unique to her. Other Union Cold Storage vessels under Blue Star management bore Blue Star livery.
1939 Renamed *Elizabeth Brodstone*.
1946 Sold to Gaselee & Son; renamed *Vespa*. Thames service.

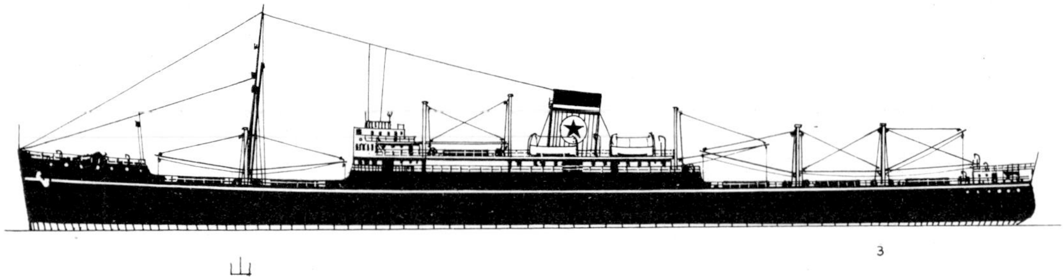

IMPERIAL STAR (I), NEW ZEALAND STAR (I)

43 **IMPERIAL STAR (I)**
B 1935 Harland & Wolff, Belfast. **T** 12,427g, 7,672n.
D 543 (165.51) oa, 524.2 (159.78) x 70.4 (21.46) x 32.9 (9.84).
E Tw scr, oil; 4 stroke B&W type sgl acting 2 x 10 cyls 1,631 NHP, 17 kts. By builder.
H Steel. 3 dks +pt 4th. F 72 (21.94). B 193 (58.83). C 560,000 cu ft (15,857.5 cu m) refrig. 20 derricks and 1 x 50 ton at foremast. **P** 12.
1934 Oct 9: Launched by the push of a button from New Zealand by Lord Bledisloe, Governor General. Wireless transmission was used to activate the launching rams. Lady Vestey did the actual naming.
1935 Jan: Entered service. She and her consorts were capable of maintaining a service speed of 17 knots.
1940 Oct: Attacked by a surfaced U-boat, which was intercepting a small ship at the time. *Imperial Star's* first shell in reply was close and the second so near that the submarine crash dived. When the submarine next surfaced her prey was out of range. Both ships escaped.
1941 Jan: Transferred to Frederick Leyland & Co. March 12: Bombed and hit in Brocklebank Dock, Liverpool. Sept: Sailed from the U.K. in a convoy of 9 fast 15 knot ships for Malta, Operation Halbard, carrying cargo and 2,600 troops. From Gibraltar the escort consisted of 3 battleships, *Prince of Wales, Nelson* and *Rodney*, the aircraft carrier *Ark Royal*, 5 cruisers and 18 screening destroyers.
Sept 27: 20.32; A torpedo from attacking Italian hit aft blowing off the rudder and both screw. The destroyer *Heythorp* took off 300 troops and some of the crew while the destroyer *Oribi* put a line aboard and commenced to tow the 20,000 dwt ship. The pair went round in circles and at one stage *Imperial Star* was towing the straining *Oribi* backwards. Worse *Imperial Star* was settling by the stern. Sept 28: 01.20; *Oribi* gave up. She was no longer even moving the deadweight ship. After taking off the remaining 141 she lashed 3 depth charges to the side of the stricken vessel and hit them with her gunfire. During this period the attacking Italian submarine *Adua* was sunk.

44 **NEW ZEALAND STAR (I)**
Details as *Imperial Star* (43) except **T** 12,436g, 7,677n.
D 542.9ft (165.47m).
1934 Nov 22: Launched for the parent company.
1935 March: Entered service to New Zealand.
1940 Transferred to Frederick Leyland & Co. She was extremely fortunate to serve throughout the war without serious incident.
1950 Moved across to Lamport & Holt; same name and service.
1953 Transferred to another Vestey concern: Booth S.S. Co. These changes in ownership were either fiscal to use up depreciation allowances or they signified a change of route service but in this case a name change generally followed. Thus *New Zealand Star* continued unchanged and never wore either L & H or Booth colours.
1967 Aug: Broken up by Shimabun K.K. at Etajima Island near Kure. At this time she bore Crusader Shipping Co's colours for N.Z.—Japan service.

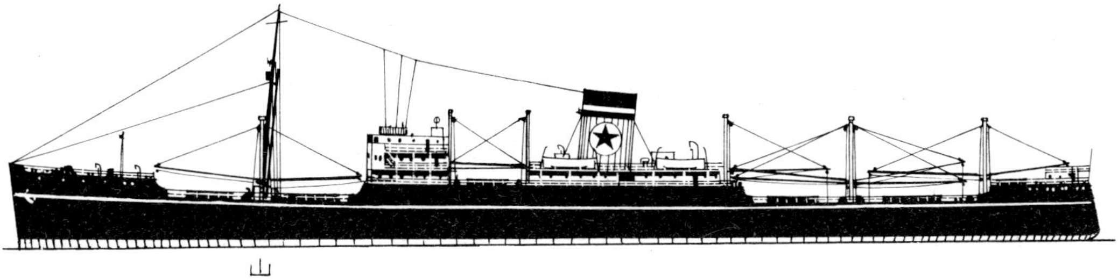

AUSTRALIA STAR (I), DUNEDIN STAR (I), EMPIRE STAR (II), SYDNEY STAR (I)

45 **AUSTRALIA STAR (I)**

B 1935 Harland & Wolff, Belfast. **T** 12,614g, 8,001n, 11,488 dwt.
D 542 (165.2) oa, 524.2 (159.78) x 70.4 (21.45) x 32.3 (9.84).
E Tw scr, oil, 2 stroke B & W type dbl acting 2 x 6 cyls, 2,463 NHP; 17 kts. By builder. Fuel 2,313 tons.
H Steel. 3 + part 4th dks. F 72 (21.94). B 193 (58.83). P 59 (17.98). C 749,000 cu ft (21,209.4 cu m) refrig. **P** 12.
1935 Jan 8: Launched. This was the third of the *Imperial Star* class but she emerged not only with a poop but also split bridge deck superstructure. Ownership was Frederick Leyland & Co with Blue Star management. April: Delivered for New Zealand service.
1941 May 3: Damaged by incendiaries during the Liverpool 'May Blitz' but not put out of commission.
1944 Collided with and sank the steamer *Hindu* in darkness when in convoy. She picked up the survivors and put back into Cristobal for repairs.
1950 Transferred to Blue Star Line Ltd ownership.
1964 June 15: Arrived at Faslane for scrapping by Shipbreaking Industries Ltd.

46 **DUNEDIN STAR (I)**

B 1936 Cammell Laird & Co, Birkenhead. **T** 12,891g, 8,020n, 13,000 dwt.
D 551 (167.94) oa, 530 (161.54) x 70.4 (21.46) x 32.2 (9.81).
E Tw scr, oil; 2 x 20 cyls, 12,000 BHP, 17 kts. By Sulzer Diesel, Winterthur. **H** Steel. 1 + shelter dk. **P** 12.
1935 Oct 29: Launched.
1936 Feb: Delivered to Union Cold Storage Co.
1941 Sept: Took part in the Malta convoy 'Operation Halbard' in which *Imperial Star* (43) was sunk. Arrived safely.
1942 Nov 29: Enroute Liverpool—Saldanha Bay struck a submerged object off the west coast of Africa.

In sinking condition the ship was beached in heavy surf 500 yards off shore on the notorious Skeleton Coast. Wilhelmsen's *Temeraire* and Manchester Liners' *Manchester Division* arrived only to find that 63 survivors had reached shore and were stranded. They were able to take off the remaining 53. The Cape Town tug *Sir Charles Elliot* next came on the scene but because of the surf was unable to reach those ashore. In this attempt the tug was herself wrecked 40 miles down the coast when she ran out of coal. The minesweeper *Nerine* arrived and attempted to float food ashore but left on December 4 due to lack of fuel. Supplies were next dropped by a bomber which then attempted to land but became bogged down in the sand. Rescue set off from Windhoek, 600 miles away, in a convoy of 8 vehicles which left on December 2. When H.M.S.A.S. *Nerine* reappeared she had a surf boat and rescue experts with her.

Dec 10: The surf boat managed to take off 17 persons before it was wrecked. They next used a ship's lifeboat to pull 11 more, including 2 of her own crew, to safety before leaving with 26 survivors.

Dec 12: The land convoy, which had been bogged down in unexplored territory was four miles away and a second convoy was 40 miles behind.

Dec 24: The convoy finally arrived back at Windhoek.

1943 Jan: Salvage of *Dunedin Star's* mail and vital supplies commenced by the ex-trawler *Crassula*. The ship's back broke and in the end was abandoned.

1951 Brass and other valuable metals were salvaged from the largely intact wreck which was now sinking into the sand.

47 **EMPIRE STAR (II)**

Details as 46 except: **T** 12,656g, 9,187n. **D** 543 (165.5). **H** P 64 (19.51).

1935 Sept 26: Launched for Frederick Leyland & Co. Blue Star Line managers. Dec: Entered service.

1942 Feb 6: The Japanese commenced their attack on Singapore. Feb 12: *Empire Star*, escorted by H.M.S. *Durban* and H.M.S. *Kedah* left Singapore for Batavia. At 8.50am, at the exit to the Durian Strait, the ship was attacked by 6 dive bombers and hit three times. 57 bombers, in relays, continued high level attacks. During the engagement 16 were killed and 67 wounded out of an under-estimated 2,160 aboard. One bomber was shot down and another left trailing smoke. The ship reached Batavia and went on to Australia. Repairs were effected at Fremantle.

1942 Oct 18: 6.43pm, enroute Liverpool—Cape Town with a general cargo and a complement of 19 passengers the ship was torpedoed by *U-615* in the engine room. The vessel was in mid-Atlantic, off the Azores, in storm conditions. All the survivors pulled away from the ship, which appeared not to be sinking but two more torpedoes hit her simultaneously and the ship up-ended and sank immediately. An overcrowded lifeboat, containing Captain Capon and 37 crew was never seen again but two boat loads were picked up by H.M.S. *Black Swan*. The only other casualties were 4 engine room staff. One mystery remains: after the sinking there was a tremendous detonation underwater and, unusually, the U-boat did not surface. It certainly was not U-615 which was sunk in the Caribbean in the following year.

48 **SYDNEY STAR (I)**

Details as *Australia Star* (45) except: **B** 1936. **T** 12,696g, 9,225n.
D 542.8 (165.44). **E** 2 x 6 cyl Burmeister & Wain type by builder.
H 1 dk + shelter dk + pt 3 and 4th dks. **P** 64 (19.51).

1936 Jan 11: Launched for Frederick Leyland & Co; Blue Star as managers. July: Commissioned.

1939 Aug: Carried the Prime Minister of Queensland to the official opening of the Outer Harbour, Port Mackay.

1941 July 24: While serving on Malta convoy duty *Sydney Star* was torpedoed at night by E-boats off Pantellaria. Apart from supplies she was carrying 460 troops who were transferred in the space of 40 minutes to the escorting destroyer *Nestor*. The ship was left with only a skeleton crew and at dawn her commander, Captain Horn, instructed those aboard on the handling of the ani-aircraft guns. The first air attack began at 5.30am and was beaten off. Another at 7.30am was repulsed. The third, at 6.35am, a high level bombing run, missed by only 30ft. Listing badly and down by the head the ship, making ony 5 knots, cut through the mine fields and made port safely with an estimated two hours to spare. The hole made by the torpedo was 40ft (12.19m) by 16ft (4.87m) and took, starting Aug 18, four months for Malta Dockyards to repair.

1950 Owned by Blue Star Line Ltd.

1967 Sold at Liverpool to Embajada Cia Nav S.A. R/n *Kent* for her final laden voyage from Rotterdam to the Far East. Aug 11: Arrived at Kaohsiung in tow from Hong Kong for breaking up.

MELBOURNE STAR (I), BRISBANE STAR, AUCKLAND STAR (I), WELLINGTON STAR (I), ADELAIDE STAR (I)

49 **MELBOURNE STAR (I)**
Details as *Australia Star* (45) except: **B** 1936 Cammell Laird & Co, Birkenhead. **T** 12,806g, 7,964n. **D** 548.8ft (167.27m) oa. **E** By Sulzer, Winterthur, installed by builder. 2 x 10 cyls. sgl acting. **H** 2 dks pt 3 + 4th. F 70 (21.34). B 202 (61.57). P 83 (25.3).
1936 July 7: Launched. This ship introduced the longer poop. Nov: Entered service for Union Cold Storage Co Ltd, Blue Star as managers.
1940 Oct 5: 450 miles west of Ireland the ship was attacked by Focke-Wulfe bombers. One direct hit failed to explode and machine gunning killed one.
1941 July 24: Damaged by E-boat attack enroute to Malta but reached Valetta safely although one bomb hit failed to explode.
1942 Aug 12: Took part in Operation Pedestal to Malta. This was the most heavily protected of all and included the epic of the tanker *Ohio*. *Melbourne Star* endured continuous daylight air attack and by night E-boat harrassment; she nevertheless arrived safely. At Malta the ship was festooned with camouflage nets and bomb detonating wire mesh.
1943 March 22: Departed from Liverpool via Panama for Sydney. Apr 2: 3am, torpedoed by *U-129* 480 miles from Bermuda in bad weather. The ship was laden with ammunition and high explosive which detonated blowing the ship to smithereens in one flash. 11 survivors in the water assembled together on rafts which had floated free; one drifted away never to be seen again but 38 days later an American flying boat found 4 men and was able to pick them up and flew them to Bermuda. 71 crew were lost.

50 **BRISBANE STAR**
Details as *Australia Star* (45) except: **B** 1936 Cammell Laird & Co.
T 12,791g, 7,948n **D** 551ft (167.94m) oa. **E & H** as *Melbourne Star*.
1936 Sept 16: Launched.
1937 Jan: Delivered to Union Cold Storage, Blue Star as managers.
1942 Aug 11: Took part in Operation Pedestal a Malta convoy of 14 ships that was escorted by the battleships *Nelson* and *Rodney*, the aircraft carriers *Victorious*, *Indomitable*, *Furious* and *Eagle* plus covering cruisers and destroyers. A torpedo attack blew off *Brisbane Star's* bow and making barely 3 knots the ship put into Susa, Tunisia. Despite being classed as unseaworthy the ship left port and escorted by relays of Spitfires gained Malta. She was one of only 5 ships to do so. At this time she was owned by Frederick Leyland & Co Ltd.
1943 Repaired with a bow that was cut away at 45° to the waterline from the stem midpoint making her easily identified.
1950 Transferred to Lamport & Holt; same name and management.
1958 Aug: Took the first postwar refrigerated sailing from Southampton after the rebuilding of the destroyed cold store.
1959 Reverted to Blue Star ownership.
1963 July: Sold to Margalante Cia Nav S.A. Panama; renamed *Enea*.
1965 Oct 15: Departed Rotterdam loaded for Hong Kong, thence to Osaka for breaking up.

51 **AUCKLAND STAR (I)**
Details as *Australia Star* (45) except: **B** 1939 **T** 13,212g, 7,960n.
1939 June 20: Launched for Union Cold Storage Co Ltd. Blue Star as managers. Australian service.
1940 July 28: 0400; torpedoed by *U-99* (Kretschmer) 80 miles off the coast of Ireland during her first inbound voyage from Townsville. After the ship had been abandoned a second and then a third torpedo struck and she sank immediately. The crew of 74 reached Ireland in the lifeboats.

52 **WELLINGTON STAR (I)**
Details as 51 except: **T** 13,212g, 7,960n.
1939 Apr 20: Launched; same owners and service as her sister.
1940 June 16: 11.02; torpedoed by *U-101* 300 miles off Cape Finisterre; she too was on the first inward leg of her maiden voyage. 52 survivors were landed at Casablanca, having been picked up by *Pierre L-D*, Louis Dreyfus & Cie. 17 others beached their lifeboat at Figueria and reached Oporto.

53 **ADELAIDE STAR (I)**
Sister of 51 except: **B** 1940 Burmeister & Wain, Copenhagen. **T** 12,636g, 9,209n. **D** 528 (160.93) bp. **E** By builder.
1938 Feb 22: Contract signed.
1939 Dec 30: Launched.
1940 April 9: Seized during fitting out when the Germans overran Denmark. The ship therefore never served in Blue Star service although she bore Blue Star funnel colours when taken over. Nov 6: Completed as *Seeburg* for the German Navy; managed by Hamburg America Line. Nov 19: Trials then based at Gotenhafen. Used as a depot and target practice ship for the 27th U-boat flotilla.
1944 Dec 4: Mined and sunk by the Russians off Heistevnest, Danzig Bay.
1952 Raised and beached at Gdynia.
1955 Moved into Gdynia Dockyard for repair.
1957 Emerged as *Dzierzynski* for the Polish Ocean Lines' Far East service. She still retained her distinctly Blue Star Line appearance although the fcsle derricks were now goal-post.
1963 A series of minor accidents led cumulatively to her loss. Sept 16: Enroute Shanghai—Antwerp—Gdynia she collided with the small Greek steamer *Fouli* (693grt) off Ushant. Put into Brest for examination and voyage repair. On arrival at Flushing further temporary repairs were carried out and a faulty sea valve was attended to. At Antwerp *Dzierzynski* struck a pier at Baudouin Lock. The sea valve collapsed and the engine room was flooded. To remove her from the waterway she was beached at Lillo. On the falling tide a crack appeared at No 2 hatch. Oct 1: She was taken off by tugs and towed to Liefenshoek where was was again grounded at No 92 buoy. Weakened by the constant tidal strains her back broke completely and the ship was finally condemned and eventually taken in two halves to Antwerp where she was scrapped by Jef de Smedt & Co.

GEORGE SALT

54 **GEORGE SALT**
B 1936 Henry Robb & Co, Leith. **T** 77g. 9n.
D 75.6 (23.04) x 19.1 (5.82) x 8.3 (2.52).
E Sgl scr, oil, 8 cyl, 4 stroke SA, 122 NHP. 8 kts. By Mirrlees, Bickerton & Day, Stockport.
H Steel 1 dk.
1936 Tug. Completed for Blackfriars Lighterage & Cartage Co, London. Blue Star Line as

managers. She was almost immediately transferred to Frederick Leyland & Co. Virtually a sister to *Brodstone* (42).
1945 Transferred to Lamport & Holt ownership for service at Rio Grande do Sul.
1946 Sold to Cia Nav das Lagaos, Brazil. R/n *Sao Cristovao*. Based at Rio de Janeiro.
1955 Based at Rio Grande do Sul once more.
1966 Out of Lloyds Register.

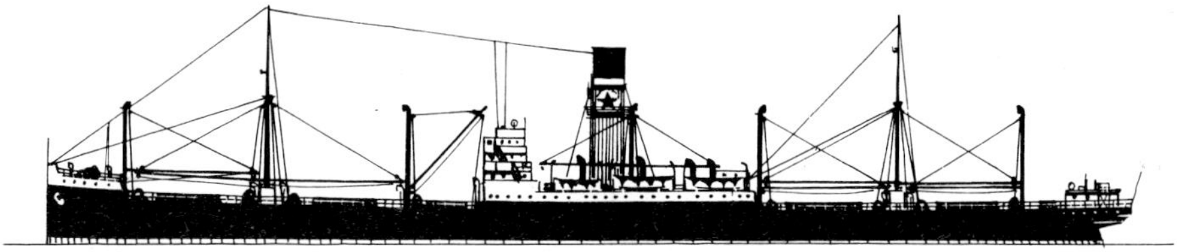

SCOTTISH STAR (I)

55 **SCOTTISH STAR (I)**
B 1917 Harland & Wolff, Govan. **T** 7,224g, 4,314n, 12,992 dwt.
D 434. (132.56) x 55.3 (16.85) x 35.2 (10.72).
E Sgl scr, quad exp, 4 cyls, 808 NHP, Stm P: 215 lb, 2 dbl ended blrs. By Harland & Wolff, Belfast. Bunkers: 2,250 tons. **H** Steel. 3 dks. F 25 (7.62). B 115 (35.05). C 636,700 cu ft (18,029.4 cu m) bale. **P** 12.
1916 Nov 7: Launched as *Millais*.
1917 May: Completed for the Liverpool, Brazil and River Plate S.N. Co, Lamport & Holt managers.
1934 Passed into Lamport & Holt ownership.
1938 Jan: To Blue Star Line. R/n *Scottish Star*.
1941 Apr 11: Bombed and damaged 400 miles north west of Ireland.
1942 Feb 2: Left Liverpool in convoy. Feb 12: Being bound for Montevideo she left the convoy to proceed independently. Feb 20: 09.50; torpedoed in the engine room by the Italian submarine *Torelli* 700 miles east north east of Trinidad. 4 killed. 09.15; the sinking ship was abandoned. H.M.S. *Diomede* picked up all but one of the lifeboats but this one reached Barbados safely on Feb 27.

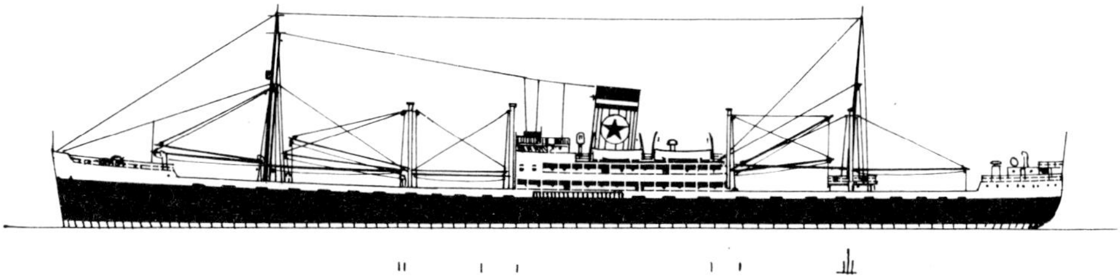

CALIFORNIA STAR (I), CANADIAN STAR (I), COLUMBIA STAR/PATAGONIA STAR/COLUMBIA STAR

56 **CALIFORNIA STAR (I)**
B 1938 Burmeister & Wain, Copenhagen. **T** 8,293g, 5,032n.
D 463.9 (141.4) oa, 447.2 (136.31) x 60.2 (18.34) x 36 (10.97).

E Sgl scr, oil, 2 stroke dbl acting, 6 cyls, 1236 NHP. 13 kts. By builder.
H Steel. 2 dks + pt 3rd F 54 (16.46). P 30 (9.14). C 465,000 cu ft (13,167 cu m). **P** 12.
1938 Aug 6: Launched for Union Cold Storage Co. The first of three 'C' class ships for the North Pacific coast service. Dec: Transferred upon completion to Frederick Leyland & Co.
1939 May: Her owners became Blue Star Line Ltd.
1940 June 12: Assigned to the Australian Government food service between Australia and the Middle East supplying her own troops in the area. During this year the mainmast of all three was removed and replaced by a pole mast out of the port bridgefront derrick post.
1943 Mar 4: Torpedoed by a spread of four from *U-515* when in convoy 380 miles west of the Azores bound for Liverpool. The third torpedo burst under No 2 lifeboat as it was being launched killing everyone in it. Another lifeboat made Flores but 51 out of the 74 aboard were lost.

57 **CANADIAN STAR (I)**
Details as 56 except: **B** 1939.
1938 Oct 20: Launched as *Canadian Star* for Union Cold Storage Co. This ship was initally ordered as *Canada Star* the reason for the change, which was out of line with the others, is not known.
1939 Feb: Completed for Union Cold Storage but allocated to Frederick Leyland & Co prior to completion only to move to Blue Star before the end of the year.
1941 July 19-20: At midnight the ship was missed by two torpedoes from *U-203* 650 miles off Lands End enroute for Auckland. The submarine surfaced and commenced damaging shellfire but the accuracy of *Canadian Star's* reply drove off her pursuer.
1943 Mar 8: Left New York in the 42 ship convoy *HX 229* which was attacked for three days west of Newfoundland by a U-boat pack. March 18: The vessel became the 9th casualty when, in gale conditions, two torpedoes from *U-221* struck No 2 hold. There were no casualties at this stage but of the 22 passengers and 69 crew only 59 were picked up by the corvettes *Anemone* and *Pennywort*. The 32 lost were swept away by ferocious seas.

58 **COLUMBIA STAR (I)/PATAGONIA STAR (I)/COLUMBIA STAR (I)**
Details as *California Star* (56) except: **B** 1939.
1939 Feb 15: Launched. for Blue Star Line. May: Delivered.
1950 Transferred to Lamport & Holt; same name. By now the mainmast had been removed and the steaming light transferred to a small tripod at the forefront of the funnel top. Blue Star remained managers.
1953 Renamed *Dryden* for the South American service.
1955 Renamed *Patagonia Star* owned by Lamport & Holt Line Ltd. Blue Star colours.
1957 Became *Columbia Star*; still Lamport & Holt. On Blue Star routes.
1959 Passed back into Blue Star Line ownership.
1963 Again renamed *Dryden* but owned by Blue Star; managed Lamport & Holt. Their colours.
1966 Ownership passed back to Lamport & Holt.
1968 Nov 10: Arrived from Shanghai at Kaohsiung for scrapping by Yung Tai Steel & Iron Works Co. The ship was a typical example of the interplay of both names and ownership practised by the Vestey group.

EMPIRE STAR

59 **EMPIRE STAR (III)**
B 1946 Harland & Wolff, Belfast. **T** 11,085g, 7,027n, 21,550 disp.
D 540.5 (164.74) oa, 521.4 (158.92) x 70.5 (21.49) x 30.9 (9.42).
E Tw scr, oil, 2 x 8 cyls B&W type 2 stroke dbl acting, 16,000 BHP, 17 kts.
By Harland & Wolff, Govan. Fuel 2,419 tons.
H Steel. 2 dks + shelter dk + pt 4th. F 68 (20.73). B 196 (59.74). 6 holds.
C 443,159 cu ft (12,548.9 cu m) refrig. Equipped with a swimming pool. 22 derricks.
P 36 1st in accommodation below the bridge. 92 tst along the bridgedeck.
1946 Mar 4: Launched as *Empire Mercia*, one of a class of four ships built to Shaw, Savill & Albion design. Owned by the Admiralty with Ministry of Transport as the intended managers. Dec: Completed as *Empire Star* for Frederick Leyland & Co. Blue Star Line as managers. The ship was fitted with remoted thermometers in each hold that could be read from the bridge. Previously readings had to be taken manually. They became standard in refrigerated vessels thereafter. Glasgow—South Africa—Australia service.
1950 Transferred to Lamport & Holt ownership but continued as a unit of the Blue Star fleet. Pass. 12.
1971 Oct 16: Arrived at Kaohsiung for breaking up by Long Jong Industrials.

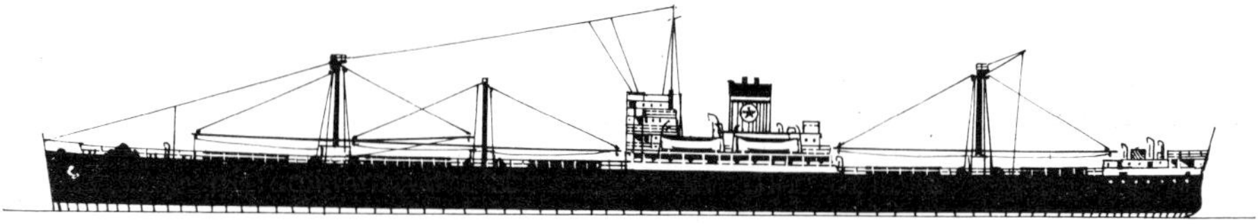

GOTHIC STAR (II)/ NELSON STAR/PATAGONIA STAR (II), SAXON STAR (II)

60 **GOTHIC STAR (II)/NELSON STAR/PATAGONIA STAR (II)**
B 1943 Harland & Wolff, Belfast. **T** 7,356g, 5,126n. 9,290 dwt.
D 448 (136.55) oa, 431.4 (131.49) x 57.3 (17.46) x 33.6 (10.24).
E Sgl scr, oil, 6 cyls, B&W type, 2 stroke sgl acting, 2,650 BHP, 12 kts. By builder (Govan).
H Steel. 2 dks. **C** 437,000 cu ft (12,374.5 cu m) bale. Fuel: 934 tons.
1942 Aug 25: Launched.
1943 Jan: Completed as *Empire Castle*, Ministry of War Transport, Federal S.N. as managers.
1944 Blue Star Line Ltd became her managers.
1946 May: Acquired. June: R/n *Gothic Star*.
1947 As the names of the fleet came to be identified with the routes served the traditional names were discarded, being on the New Zealand run the ship was renamed *Nelson Star*. Fidded foremast top added.
1958 With her transfer to the South American route she was renamed *Patagonia Star*.
1961 May: Sold to Gregory Maritime Ltd, r/n *Birini*. Operated by G.A. Theodorou & Sons (Shipping) Co, Cyprus.
1970 Feb: Acquired by Angila Shipping Co, r/n *Byzantium*. Sept: Laid up at Gibraltar with engine trouble. Assessed as beyond economical repair.
1971 July 31: Arrived in tow at Puerto de Santa Maria, Bay of Cadiz, and broken up on the beach.

61 **SAXON STAR (II)**
As 60 except: **B** 1942. **T** 7,355g, 5,120n. **D** 450.4 (137.28).
1942 May 28: Launched as *Empire Strength*, M.O.W.T., with Blue Star as managers. Dec: Entered service.
1946 March: Acquired and renamed *Saxon Star*, Frederick Leyland & Co.
1950 Transferred to Lamport & Holt. Same name and service.

1954 Inter-group transfer to Booth Line.
1959 Back to Blue Star; general duties according to need.
1961 Sold to D. L. Street. R/n *Redbrook*. Privately owned; tramping.
1965 Sold to Hegif Cia Nav S.A. Greece. Renamed *Evangelia*.
1968 Oct 15: Enroute Rijeka—Constantia the ship drove ashore at Constantia and was wrecked.

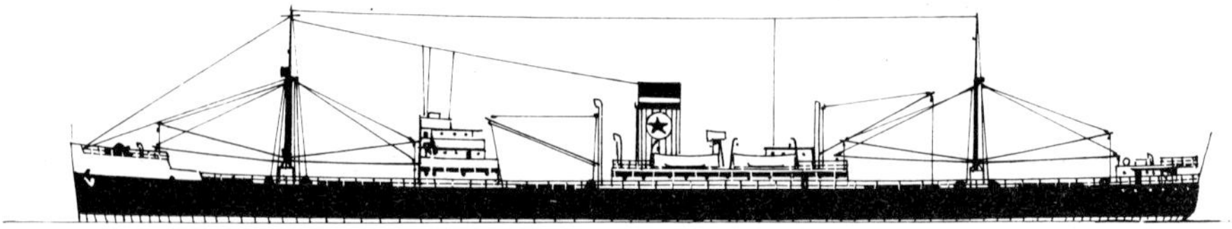

IONIC STAR (II)/NAPIER STAR (II)

62 **IONIC STAR (II)/NAPIER STAR (II)**
B 1942 Barclay Curle & Co, Whiteinch. **T** 7,166g, 4,279n.
D 431.3 (131.46) oa, 418 (127.41) x 57.4 (17.5) x 34.2 (10.42).
E Sgl scr, oil, 4 cyls, Doxford design, 2 stroke sgl acting. 10 kts. By builder.
H Steel. 2 dks. F 36 (10.97). C 368,000 cu ft (10,420.6 cu m) refrig.
1942 Aug 26: Launched as *Empire Highway*, M.O.W.T., Blue Star managers. Oct: Delivered.
1943 July 27: Damaged by bomb attack off Lisbon bound for Buenos Aires. Repaired at Gibraltar.
1946 Aug: Acquired by Union Cold Storage Co Ltd. R/n *Ionic Star*. Short funnel.
1947 Jan: Given the name *Napier Star* to conform with the new destinational nomenclature. Taller funnel fitted (as drawn).
1949 Transferred to Frederick Leyland ownership.
1950 Passed into Lamport & Holt ownership without other change.
1953 Moved across to Booth Line; she was the first to be so transferred but not the last.
1959 Reverted to Blue Star Line Ltd.
1963 March 31: Arrived at Timaru to become the 100th Blue Star call.
1965 July 21: Grounded enroute Rio Gallegos—London at Bahia Potrero, Punta del Este, Uruguay. Aug 19: Refloated. Aug 21: Drydocked at Montevideo. Oct: Declared to be a constructive total loss and put up for sale.
1966 Sold to Urria & Cia for scrap; attempts to sell her for further trading failed. It was two years before demolition commenced.

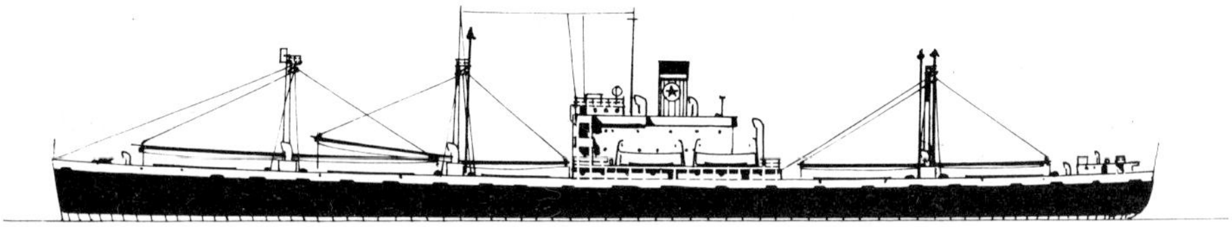

OREGON STAR (II), PACIFIC STAR (II)

63 **OREGON STAR (II)**
B 1944 New England Ship Building Co, Portland Maine. **T** 7,283g, 4,497n. 9,740 dwt.
D 441.7 (134.63) oa, 423.9 (129.2) x 57 (17.37) x 34.8 (10.61).
E Sgl scr, tpl exp, 3 cyls, 2,500 IHP, Stm P: 240 lb, 2 water tube blrs. 10½ kts.
By Harrisburg Mchy Corp, Harrisburg, Pa.
H Steel. 2 dks. 3 masts. C 426,500 cu ft (12,077.2 cu m)g. Fuel: 1,251 tons.

1944 Jan 31: Launched as *Samannan*, American War Shipping Administration. Placed on bareboat charter with Ministry of War Transport, Blue Star as managers.
1947 Apr: Acquired for £135,000 by Blue Star Line. R/n *Oregon Star* for the north Pacific routes.
1952 March: Transferred to Lamport & Holt; r/n *Laplace*.
1953 Apr: Sold to San Panteleimon Cia Nav S.A., Costa Rica. R/n *San Panteleimon*.
1959 Passed into Greek registry.
1963 July 16: Enroute Morocco—China she had to be beached near to Galle, Sri Lanka, with engine room flooded. Refloated and repaired.
1967 Apr 20: Arrived at Yokosuka for breaking up by Matsukura Kaiji. This followed damage sustained when she broke adrift in a gale at Kobe and struck a stone pier.

64 **PACIFIC STAR (II)**
Sister of 63 except: **B** Bethlehem Fairfield Shipyard, Baltimore, Ohio. **T** 7,259g, 4,486n. **E** By Worthington Pump & Mchy Co, Hamilton, Ontario.
1944 Jan 15: Launched as *Samnid* by the film star Mary Pickford. Operated similarly as her sister.
1947 July: Joined Blue Star as *Pacific Star* for north Pacific service.
1950 Oct: Suffered minor fire damage in dock at Cardiff.
1951 Transferred to Lamport & Holt. R/n *Lalande*. Sold after a few weeks to S.A. Importazione Carboni e Nav. (SAICEN). R/n *Ninfea*.
1959 Became *Nan Hai 147* of the China Ocean Shipping Co (COSCO) , Shanghai.
1979 Renamed *Hong Qi 147*; registered at Canton. Same owners.
1987 Still in the register.

Note: Blue Star were also the managers, but never the owners of *Saminver* and *Samtay*. Both latterly carried the Blue Star funnel over a grey livery. *Saminver* carried 450 vehicles and 500 troops to the Normandy Arronmanches beach in June 1944.

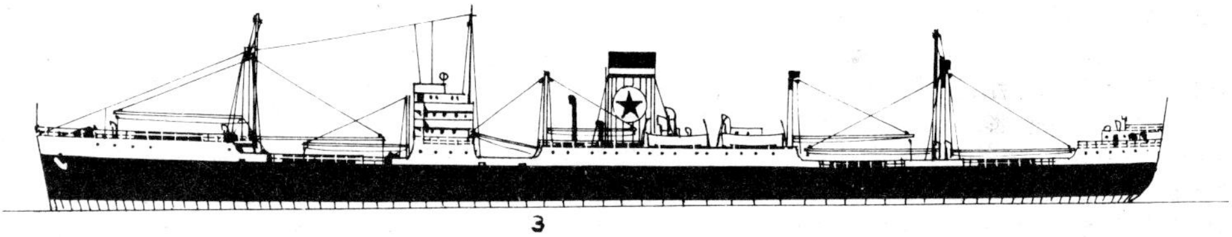

3

A. ROYAL STAR (II)/CALEDONIA STAR

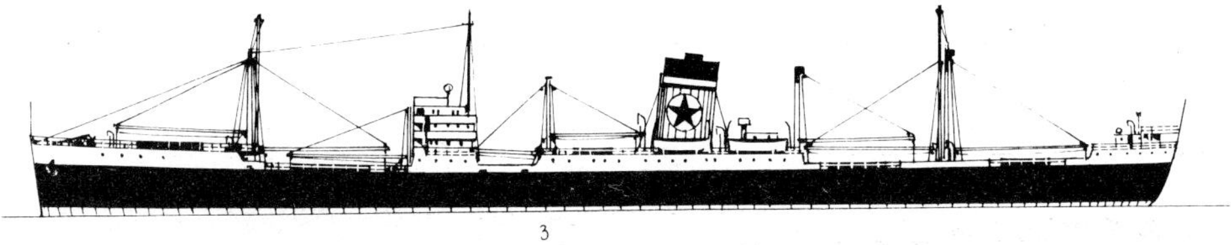

3

B. CALEDONIA STAR

65 **ROYAL STAR (II)/CALEDONIA STAR**
B 1942 Greenock Dockyard, Greenock. **T** 9,205g, 5,065n, 10,493dwt.
D 487.6 (148.62) oa, 463.8 (141.37) x 63 (19.2) x 38.1 (11.61).
E Sgl scr, tpl exp, 3 cyls and LP turb. 10½ kts. By J. G. Kincaid. Fuel 1,166 tons oil.
H Steel. 3 dks. F 69 (21.03). Fore B 22 (6.71). After B 102 (31.1). P 32 (9.75).
C 300,000 cu ft (8495.1 cu m) refrig, 248,000 cu ft (7,022 cu m) g.
1942 July 29: Launched as *Empire Wisdom*. Ministry of War Transport. Clan Line as managers. Nov: Completed. Thin wartime funnel.

1945 Transferred to Blue Star management with an option to purchase.
1946 Sept: Acquired by Union Cold Storage. R/n *Royal Star*. Squat funnel. (A).
1961 Oct: Converted into a motor ship by Bremer Vulkan, Vegesack. 2 x 5 cyls, 9,000 BHP, 12½ kts. Fatter modern funnel (as drawn B).
1962 Emerged as *Caledonia Star*, Blue Star Line owned.
1971 Dec 9: At Kaohsiung from Osaka. Scrapped by Dah Yung Steel.

TUSCAN STAR (II)/TIMARU STAR (I)

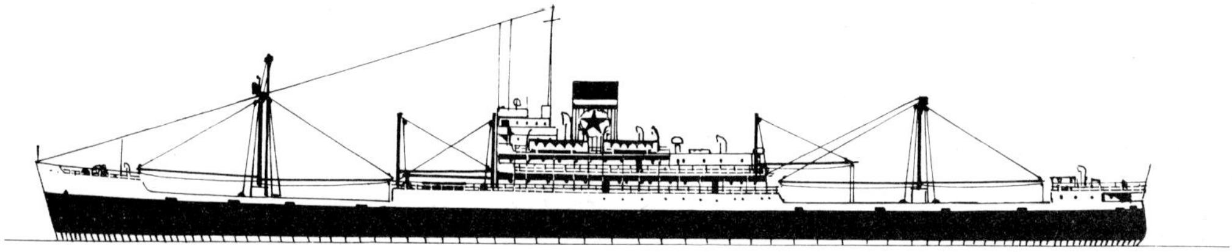

A. CALIFORNIA STAR (II)

66 **TUSCAN STAR (II)/TIMARU STAR (I)/CALIFORNIA STAR (II)**
B 1945 Harland & Wolff, Belfast. **T** 7,930g, 4,686n, 9,640 dwt.
D 474.2 (144.53) oa, 457.3 (139.28) x 63.3 (19.29) x 35 (10.67).
E Sgl scr, oil, 8 cyl Burmeister & Wain 2 stroke dbl acting; 14 kts. By builder. Fuel 1,506 tons.
H Steel. 2 dks + pt 3rd. F 48 (14.63). B 176 (53.64). C 421,260 cu ft (11,928.8 cu m) ins. 18 derricks.
P 35 1948: 12
1945 Oct: Completed as *Empire Clarendon*, a sister of *Empire Abercorn* which became *Rakaia*, New Zealand S. Co, for the Ministry of War Transport with P. & O. S.N. Co as managers.
1946 Nov: Acquired by Frederick Leyland & Co; Blue Star as managers.
1947 Renamed *Tuscan Star*.
1948 Aug 28: Renamed *Timaru Star* to conform with New Zealand route namings.
1950 Transferred to Lamport & Holt.
1954 Oct: Stood by the burning *Trojan Star* (see 29).
1958 Transferred to the North American Pacific coast route; renamed *California Star*. (66A)
1959 Reverted to Blue Star Line ownership.
1967 Placed on the New Zealand service.
1968 Mar: Laid up in the River Blackwater.
June 22: Left London on her final voyage to New Zealand.
1969 Apr 21: Sold for $280,000 and arrived at Kaohsiung for breaking up by Tsuan Yan Steel. She was the last Blue Star ship to have bridge wing cabs.

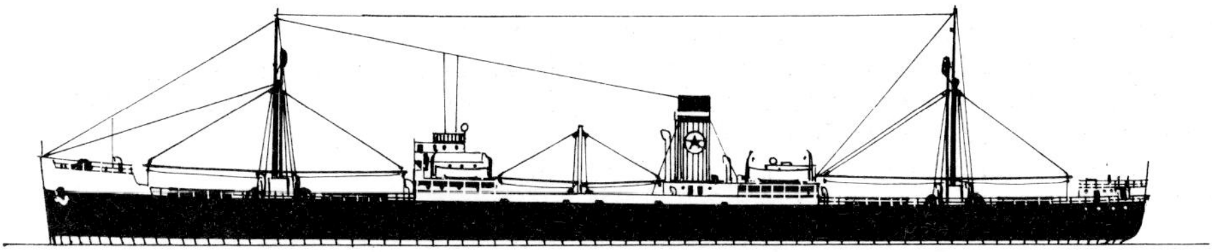

CELTIC STAR (II), OREGON STAR (III), CORRIENTES

67 **CELTIC STAR (II)**
B Vickers Armstrong, Barrow. **T** 7,046g, 4,906n, 9,740 dwt.
D 447.6 (136.42) oa, 432.5 (131.83) x 56.2 (17.13) x 34.2 (10.42).
E Sgl scr, tpl exp, 3 cyls, 549 NHP, 2 sgl ended blrs, Stm P: 22 lb. 10½ kts.
By J. G. Kincaid. Fuel 1,250 tons.
H Steel. 2 dks. F 39 (11.89). C 426,500 cu ft (12,077 cu m) bale.
1942 May 18: Launched as *Empire Galahad* for the Ministry of War Transport, Blue Star Line as managers. July: In service.
1946 Apr: Became part of the Blue Star fleet by purchase; renamed *Celtic Star*.
1947 Transferred to Lamport & Holt; became *Murillo*. Their colours.
1952 Apr: Sold to Industriale Marittima S.p.A. Renamed *Bogliasco*.
1963 Acquired by Ocean Shipping & Enterprises (Panama) S.A; became *Ocean Peace*.
1967 Sept 13: Arrived for breaking up at Kaohsiung, Taiwan.

68 **OREGON STAR (III)**
Details as *Celtic Star* (67) except: **B** 1942 Chas Connell & Co, Scotstoun.
T 7,018g, 4.099n. **D** 446.3 (136.03) oa, 431.3 (131.46) **E** By D. Rowan & Co, Glasgow.
1942 Sept 1: Launched as *Empire Geraint*, M.O.W.T., Royal Mail Line as managers. Funnel slightly thinner.
1943 Mar 7: Collided with Royal Mail's *Andes* at Southampton. Both needed repairs.
1945 Jan: Managed by Lamport & Holt. Mar 6: Damaged by a torpedo from *U-1302* off Milford Haven. Unloaded at Swansea and then light to Newport News, USA, for repairs.
1946 Jan: Acquired by Lamport & Holt; r/n *Millais*.
1952 Transferred to Blue Star Line. R/n *Oregon Star*; north Pacific run.
1954 May: Disposed of to Iris Shipping & Trading Corp; r/n *Captayannis*.
1960 Sold to Paleocrassis Bros, Piraeus; same name.
1962 Feb 28: Grounded by Goeree Lightship, Holland bound for Rotterdam. Floated off with bottom damage. Broken up later in the year by Frank Rijsdijk at Hendrik-ido-Ambacht.

69 **CORRIENTES (OAKLAND STAR)**
Details as *Celtic Star* (67) except: **B** 1944 Short Bros, Sunderland.
T 7,078g, 4,756n. **D** 446.5 (136.09) oa, 431 (131.37).
E By N. E. Marine Eng Co, Newcastle. **H** F 40 (12.19).
1944 Dec 24: Launched as *Empire Cromer*, M.O.W.T., Donaldson Bros as managers.
1945 April: Entered service.
1946 March: Acquired by Donaldson's and renamed *Corrientes*.
1954 March: Technically taken over when Blue Star absorbed the Donaldson north Pacific route. She was to have become *Oakland Star* but being surplus to requirements she was put up for sale. Never wore Blue Star colours nor did she see service with them. She is omitted from many fleet lists and is here for record purposes only.
1955 Became *Inchmay*, Williamson & Co, Hong Kong.
1966 Sold to the National Shipping Corp. of Pakistan. R/n *Kaukhali*.
1968 Apr 2: Arrived at Karachi with machinery defects. Oct: Sold and scrapped by Eastern Steel at Gadani Beach (in early 1969).

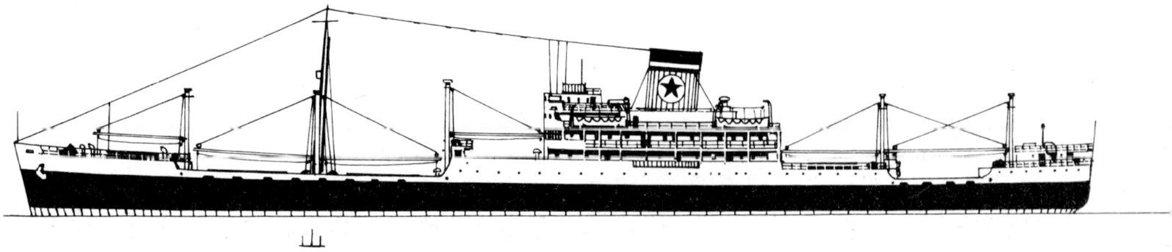

ARGENTINA STAR, BRASIL STAR, URUGUAY STAR, PARAGUAY STAR

70 **ARGENTINA STAR**
B 1947 Cammell Laird & Co, Birkenhead. **T** 10,716g, 6,328n, 11,600 dwt.
D 502.8 (153.25) oa, 478.4 (145.82) x 68.3 (20.81) x 35.9 (10.94).
E Sgl scr, 3 ahead and 2 astern dbl reduction geared Parson's stm turbines. 2 Babcock & Wilcox water tube blrs Stm P: 480 lb at 750°F. Fuel 2,012 tons. By builder.
H Steel. 3 dks + pt 4th. F 77 (23.47). B 194 (59.13). P 49 (14.94).
C 400,000 cu ft (11,326.8 cu m) refrig. 60,000 cu ft (1,699 cu m)g.
P 60 1st in sgl and dbl cabins on bridge deck. Crew 91. There was also a Lido deck with swimming pool forward of the bridge.
1946 Sept 26: Launched.
1947 June: Completed. These four ships were replacements for the five 'A' class passenger liners lost during the war. Owned by Frederick Leyland & Co. June 14: Maiden voyage London—Lisbon—Tenerife—Rio de Janeiro—Santos—Montevideo—Buenos Aires.
1950 Transferred to Union International Co ownership; same managers.
1972 Sold to Nissho-Iwai Co Ltd, Japan. Resold to their Taiwan subsidiary. Oct 19: Arrived for scrapping at Kaohsiung by Yi Ho Steel & Iron Works.

71 **BRASIL STAR**
Details as *Argentina Star* (70) except: **T** 10,716g, 6,342n, 11,610 dwt.
1947 Mar 6: Launched. Oct 15: Maiden voyage to South America. Owned by Frederick Leyland & Co.
1950 Transferred to Union International Co.
1972 Sold, along with her sister *Argentina Star*, for demolition. Oct 10: Arrived one week before her sister, at Kaohsiung. Dec 10: Breaking up commenced by Tung Seng Steel & Iron Works.

72 **URUGUAY STAR**
Sister of 70 except: **B** 1948 **T** 10,723g, 6,330n.
1947 Oct 15: Launched. Ident: No king posts athwart foremast.
1948 May 22: M/v from Liverpool; thereafter from London. Blue Star ownership.
1972 Sold for scrap. In all the four sisters of this class made 398 round voyages to South America without a machinery breakdown of any sort. Aug 25: Arrived Kaohsiung for breaking up by Nan Feng Steel Enterprise Co. She was the first of the trio of sisters to arrive; the other two followed within days of each other in October.

73 **PARAGUAY STAR**
Details as *Argentina Star* except: **B** 1948 **T** 10,723g, 6,330n.
1947 Oct 15: Launched. Oct: Delivered; no king posts abreast foremast.
1969 Aug 12: Severe engine room damage was caused by fire while berthed at the Royal Victoria Dock, London. The blaze started in a generator and spread to an oil tank thence to the machinery space and on to the passenger accommodation. After inspection the ship was declared to be beyond economical repair. Sold to Eckhardt & Co, Hamburg. Sept 15: Left London in tow. Sept 19: Arrived. She was thus the only one of the quartet not to fulfil a full service life.

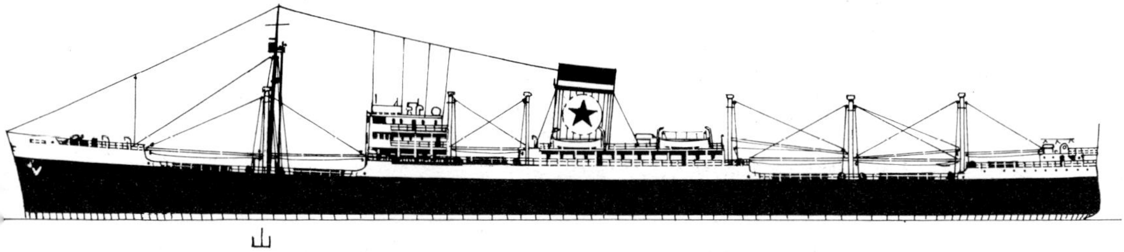

IMPERIAL STAR (II), MELBOURNE STAR (II)

74 **IMPERIAL STAR (II)**
B 1948 Harland & Wolff, Govan. **T** 13,181g, 8,113n, 13,105 dwt.
D 572.3 (174.43) oa, 549.9 (167.61) x 70.3 (21.43) x 40.7 (12.41).
E Tw scr, oil, 2 x 8 cyls, B&W type, 2 stroke dbl acting, 16,000 BHP, 17 kts. By builder.
H Steel. 3 dks. F 73 (22.25). B 208 (63.4) P 70 (21.34). Fuel 3,551 tons.
C 585,869 cu ft (1,659 cu m) refrig. Derricks 1 x 60 tons, 6 x 10 tons, 14 x 7 tons.
1947 June 17: Launched (2 days late).
1948 Mar: Completed for Union Cold Storage Co Ltd. Blue Star Line managers.
1949 The owners became the re-styled Union International Co Ltd.
1970 May: Carried the first ever cargo of frozen meat from New Zealand to Gdynia.
1971 Sept 17: Arrived at Kaohsiung to be broken up by Tung Ho Steel Enterprises.

75 **MELBOURNE STAR (II)**
Details as *Imperial Star* (74) except: **T** 13,179g, 8,091n, 13,087 dwt.
1947 Oct 2: Launched.
1948 July: Completed for Union Cold Storage Co Ltd. Blue Star Line managers.
1949 July 27: Transferred to Union International Co Ltd.
1972 Sold to Embajada Cia Nav S.A. for her final loaded voyage to the Far East. Renamed *Melbo*. June 21: Last voyage from London for Hong Kong. Aug 7: Arrived Kaohsiung for breaking up by Tung Cheng Steel & Iron Works.

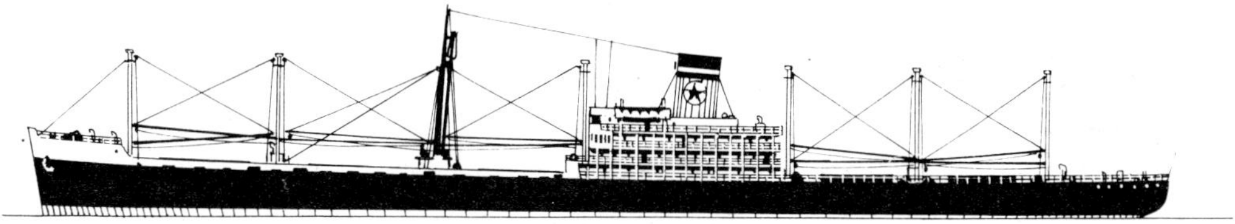

RHODESIA STAR/SOUTH AFRICA STAR

76 **RHODESIA STAR**
B 1943 Seattle-Tacoma S.B. Co, Tacoma. **T** 8,642g, 4,997n, 12,638 dwt.
D 492 (149.96) oa, 469.8 (143.19) x 69.5 (21.18) x 29.3 (8.93).
E Sgl scr, dbl reduction geared turb; 2 water-tube blrs, Stm P: 525 lb. 16 kts. By Allis-Chalmers Mfg Co, Milwaukee, Wisconsin. Fuel 1,818 tons.
H Steel. 1 dk + shelter dk + pt 3rd. F 44 (13.41). C 737,000 cu ft (20,870 cu m)g.
1943 Laid down as a standard C2-S-A1 cargo vessel. Acquired by the U.S. Navy. Oct: Completed as the Smiter Class escort carrier *Estero*. Nov 3: Transferred to the British Navy on lend-lease together with 18 similar ships. R/n H.M.S. *Premier*. Nov 11: Went to Burrard Dry Dock Co, Vancouver for modification to fit Royal Navy systems. U. S. and British fighting ships were not compatibly interchangeable.

1944 Jan 9: Entered service.
1946 Apr: Returned to the U.S. Navy. Initially laid up then converted back into a C2 type freighter by Gulf Shipbuilding Corp, Mobile and again laid up for almost two years.
1948 Acquired by Blue Star Line Ltd and r/n; *Rhodesia Star*. Ident: This ship had fcsle bulwarks; *South Africa Star* had rails.
1949 Transferred to Lamport & Holt; same name and service.
1959 Reverted to Blue Star Line.
1967 Sold to International Export Lines, C.Y. Tung group. R/n *Hongkong Knight*. Bahamas registry.
1971 Acquired by United Overseas Marine Corp S.A., Panama. Same name.
1974 Jan 1: Arrived at Kaohsiung. Feb 10: Demolition began by Yung Steel Corp.

77 **SOUTH AFRICA STAR**
Details as *Rhodesia Star* (76) except: **T** 8,529g, 4,988n, 12,400 dwt.
D 492 (149.96) oa, 470.7 (143.47) bp x 69.5 (21.18). C 732,000 cu ft (20,728 cu m) g.
1943 Feb: Completed similarly to her sister as U.S.S. *Reaper* and transferred to the British Navy as H.M.S. *Winjah*, a Smiter class carrier.
1944 March 31-May 24: Modified at Burrard Dry Dock Co, Vancouver.
1946 Reverted to the U.S. Navy and treated the same as *Rhodesia Star*.
1948 Purchased by Blue Star Line and called *South Africa Star*.
1949 Aug: Carried 400 motor cars from the Tyne to Sydney. The largest number thus far in one load.
1963 The company decided to capitalise on the heavy lift market which was steadily increasing. A 120 ton derrick was installed to the single mast. A larger one was ordered, at 250 tons, for *Rhodesia Star* but cancelled because of stability worries. It was decided to construct a new ship and the result was to be *Australia Star* (128).
1967 May 25: Arrived at Mihara, Japan, for scrapping. Broken up by Nichimen Jitsuggo K.K. commencing in June.

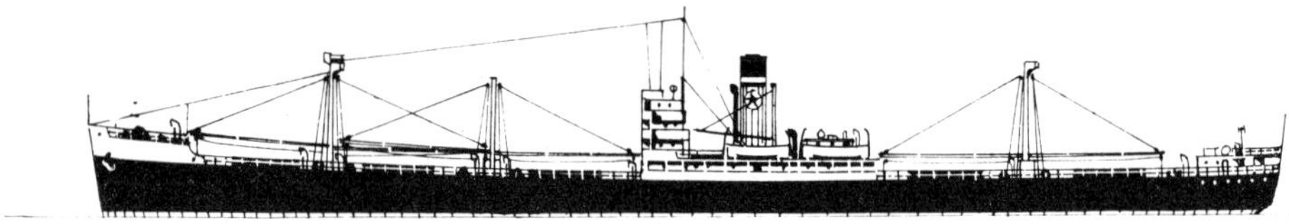

TACOMA STAR (II)

78 **TACOMA STAR (II)**
B 1944 Lithgow's Ltd, Port Glasgow. **T** 7,201g, 4,946n, 9,019 dwt.
D 447.8 (136.49) oa, 432.7 (131.89) x 56.2 (17.13) x 34.4 (10.48).
E Sgl scr, tpl exp, 3 cyls, 560 NHP, 2 sgl ended blrs. 10½ kts. By Harland & Wolff, Glasgow. Fuel 1,198 tons.
H Steel. 2 dks. F 39 (11.88). C 417,592 cu ft (11,824.9 cu m) bale. 12 derricks.
1944 Apr 20: Launched as *Empire Talisman*, Ministry of War Transport, Blue Star as managers. June: Completed.
1946 June: On bare-boat charter from the new Ministry of Transport, the replacement for the M.O.W.T.
1949 Acquired and r/n *Tacoma Star*.
1957 Passed to Lamport & Holt; r/n *Murillo*.
1959 Nov: Laid up in the Gareloch, River Clyde.
1961 Mar 16: Arrived at Vigo for demolition there.

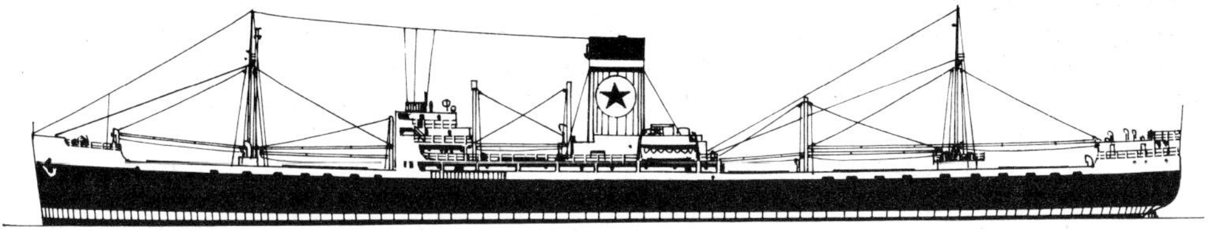

DUNEDIN STAR (II)

79 **DUNEDIN STAR (II)**
B 1950 Alex Stephen & Sons, Linthouse, Glasgow. **T** 7,322g, 4,203n, 11,200 dwt.
D 496.8 (151.42) oa, 478.7 (145.91) x 64.7 (19.72) x 28.3 (8.62).
E Sgl scr, 3 dbl reduction geared turbines, 2 water-tube blrs Stm P: 570 lb.
14 kts. By builder. Fuel 2,892 tons oil.
H Steel. 1 + shelter dk. F 39 (11.89). P 38 (11.58). Five holds and deep tank aft.
C 708,000 cu ft (20,048 cu m) bale. 1 x 50 ton derrick.
1949 Laid down as *Bolton Castle* for Moller's Trust Ltd. Allocated to the Lancashire Shipping Co, James Chambers & Co managers. Acquired by Blue Star on the stocks. This handsome ship therefore had no sisters and she made no impression on the designs of the later Blue Star vessels all of whom kept their family likeness.
1950 Apr 18: Launched as *Dunedin Star*. Sept: Delivered.
1968 Transferred to Lamport & Holt. R/n *Roland*.
1975 Owned by the Pallas Maritime Co, Cyprus. R/n *Jessica*. Her owners then became the Alligator Shipping Co.
1976 July 17: Arrived at Karachi for special survey and likely scrapping. Instead, having passed, she continued in service.
1978 May 15: Arrived from Djibouti. Sold to Carstairs & Cummings Ltd and broken up at Gadani Beach.

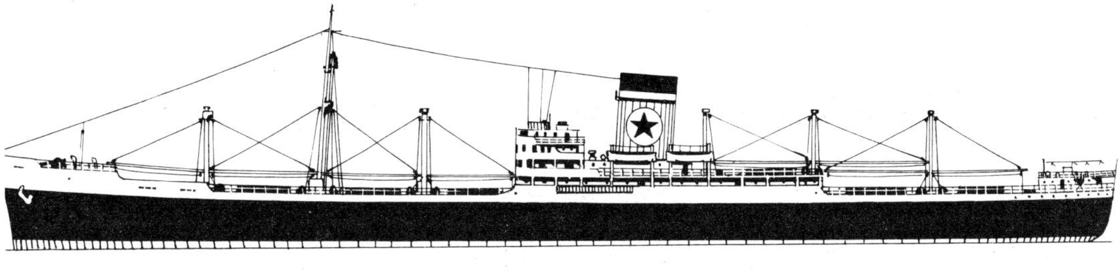

ADELAIDE STAR (II), TASMANIA STAR, WELLINGTON STAR (II), AUCKLAND STAR

80 **ADELAIDE STAR (II)**
B 1950 John Brown & Co Ltd, Clydebank. **T** 12,964g, 7,358n, 14,393 dwt.
D 573.8 (174.89) oa, 552.2 (168.25) x 72.7 (22.16) x 37.1 (11.31).
E Tw scr, oil, 2 x 6 cyls Brown-Doxford 2 stroke sgl acting, 18½ kts. By builder.
H Steel. 1 dk + shelter dk + pt 3 & 4. F 64 (19.51). C 600,000 cu ft (16,990.2 cu m) refrig. plus 378,391 cu ft (10,714 cu m) g. 1 x 60 ton derrick fitted. Equipped to carry motor cars 'tween decks. **P** 12.
1950 Aug 2: Launched; she was the largest refrigerated ship in the world and the first by John Brown for 23 years. Dec: Completed for Blue Star Line.
1964 Transferred to Lamport & Holt but continued on bare boat charter to Blue Star.
1965 Reverted to Blue Star.

1975 Mar 8: Enroute Timaru—Liverpool sustained severe damage in the engine room and to the machinery. Found to be not worth re-engining. Apr 25: Left Liverpool at the lowest economical speed for Masan, Korea. Her normal crew of 69 reduced to 34. There she was broken up by Hankook Steel.

81 **TASMANIA STAR**
Details as *Adelaide Star* (80) except: **B** 1950 Cammell Laird, Birkenhead.
T 12,605g, 7,131n, 14,500 dwt. **D** 572.3 (174.44) oa, 546.6 (166.6) bp.
E Sgl scr, 3 dbl reduction geared turbines. 2 water-tube blrs. Stm P: 550 lb.
By builder. Fuel 4,146 tons. **H** F 59 (17.98).
1950 May 31: Launched. Nov: Handed over at Liverpool. Dec: Maiden voyage with 18,000 tons of cargo which was one of the largest loads ever to leave the port.
1975 Sept 20: Arrived Kaohsiung for breaking up by G. Yuen Steel Enterprise Co.

82 **WELLINGTON STAR (II)**
Details as *Adelaide Star* except: **B** 1952. **T** 12,539g.
1952 May 7: Launched. Aug: Entered service. Her machinery duplicated that of the other John Brown vessels in the trio and in all other respects she was an exact copy.
1975 Dec: Sold at Sydney to Broad Bay Shipping Co Ltd. R/n *Hawks Bay*; Blue Star Ship Management as operators. Converted into a cattle carrier at Singapore.
1979 Sept 1: Demolition commenced at Kaohsiung by Nan Kwang Steel & Iron Co.

83 **AUCKLAND STAR (II)**
Details as *Adelaide Star* (80) except:
B 1958 Cammell Laird & Co (S.B. & Eng) Ltd, Birkenhead. **T** 11,799g, 7,013n, 15,469dwt.
D 572.34 (174.45) oa. **E** Sgl scr, stm turbines dbl reduction geared, 16,000 BHP. F 58 (17.7).
C 500,123 cu ft (14,162 cu m)ins.
1958 May 2: Launched. Oct: Entered service; owned by Salient Shipping Co (Bermuda) Ltd, Hamilton, Bermuda on bare-boat charter to Blue Star Line Ltd.
1962 Transferred to British flag.
1963 Nov: Arrived at London with the largest single cargo yet delivered from New Zealand.
1978 April 10: Final sailing from Liverpool. At this stage she had not yet been assigned for scrap. May 20: After loading at Durban the ship left for Gadani Beach for demolition. The procedure there is worth a mention. The beaching pilot orders the ship to be driven at full speed into a gap between two wrecks so that the new ship drives well up onto the sands. Those left on board are then taken off by bosun's chair to the shore. Aug: Broken up by Standard Rolling Mills.

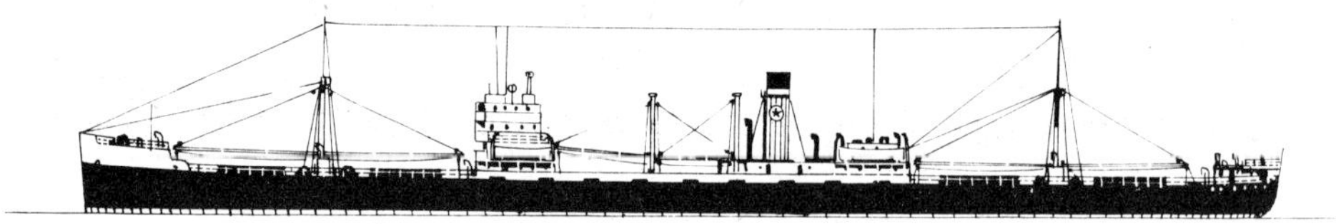

FRESNO STAR (II), VICTORIA STAR, VANCOUVER STAR

84 **FRESNO STAR (II)**
B 1944 Short Bros, Sunderland. **T** 7,053g, 4,107n, 9,655 dwt.
D 446.6 (136.12) oa, 431 (131.37) x 56.3 (17.16) x 35.2 (10.73).
E Sgl scr, tpl exp, 3 cyls, 2 sgl ended blrs, Stm P: 200 lb, 12 kts. By Harland & Wolff, Glasgow.
Fuel 1,139 tons. **H** Steel. 2 dks F 40 (12.19) C 406,000 cu ft (11,496.7 cu m) bale.
1944 Apr 11: Launched. June: Delivered as *Empire Pendennis* for the Ministry of War Transport. Ellerman Lines as managers.

1946 Apr: Acquired by Cunard White Star Ltd; renamed *Vasconia*.
1951 Sold to Blue Star Line and called *Fresno Star*.
1957 Passed on bare boat charter to Lamport & Holt; renamed *Millais*.
1960 Jan 1: Sold to Grosvenor Shipping Co, Hong Kong; became *Grosvenor Navigator*.
1966 Sept 9: Arrived for demolition at Kaohsiung by Sing Chien Yung Steel & Ironworks Co.

85 VICTORIA STAR
Details as *Fresno Star* (84) except: **B** 1943 Armstrong Whitworth & Co, Walker-on-Tyne. **T** 7,048g, 4,881n. **D** 446.3 (136.03) oa. **E** By North East Marine Eng Co.
1943 June 2: Launched. Oct: Completed as *Empire Flag*, Ministry of War Transport, managed by New Zealand Shipping Co Ltd.
1946 Apr: Acquired by Donaldson Line Ltd. R/n *Carmia*.
1954 Mar: Purchased. R/n *Victoria Star*.
1955 Oct: Sold to Williamson & Co, Hong Kong. R/n *Inchean* and operated by the Douglas S.S. Co with Douglas, Lapraik & Co as managers.
1966 Mar 26: Arrived at Osaka for scrapping.

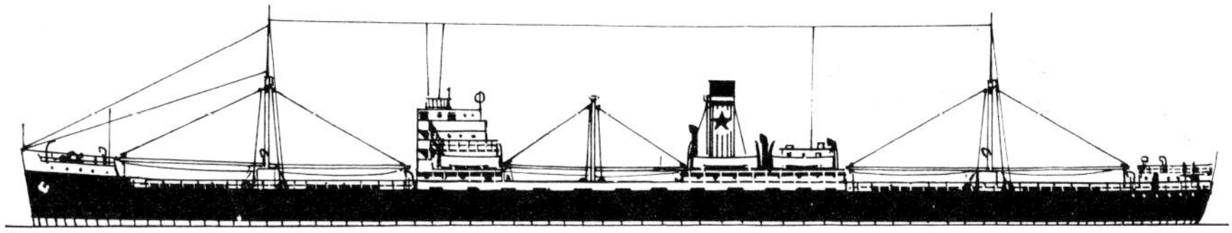

VANCOUVER STAR

86 **VANCOUVER STAR**
Details as *Fresno Star* except: **B** 1943 T 7,063g, 4,241n, 9,624 dwt. **D** 446.5 (136.1).
1942 Dec 8: Launched as *Empire Bardolph*, Ministry of War Transport.
1943 March: Completed. Donaldson Bros as managers.
1945 Sold to Lamport & Holt. R/n *Memling* in the following year.
1953 Transferred to Blue Star Line Ltd; became *Vancouver Star*.
1957 Reverted to Lamport & Holt as *Memling*.
1959 Oct: Arrived for dismantling by N. V. Simon's Metaalhandel, Flushing.

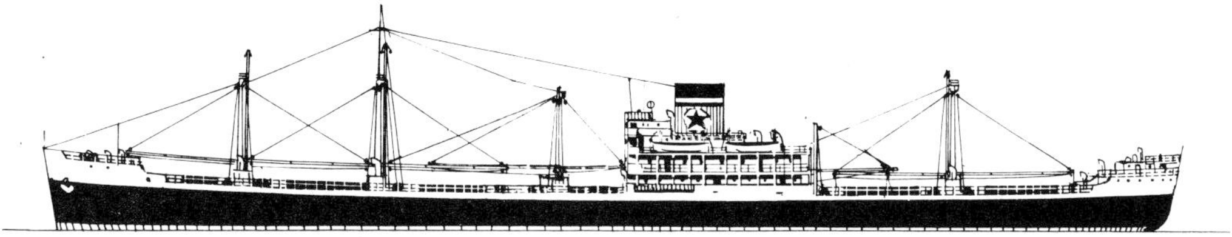

FREMANTLE STAR (I)/CATALINA STAR

87 **FREMANTLE STAR (I)/CATALINA STAR**
B 1944 Lithgow's Ltd, Port Glasgow. **T** 9,883g, 6,185n, 9,923 dwt.
D 497.4 (151.61) oa, 476 (145.08) x 64.3 (19.6) x 40 (12.19).
E Sgl scr, oil, 6 cyls, B&W type, 2 stroke dbl acting, 12½ kts. By J. G. Kincaid. Fuel 1,508 tons.
H Steel. 2 dks + pt 3rd. F 40 (12.19). P 33 (10.06). C 646,000 cu ft (18,292.8 cu m) g.
1944 Oct 6: Launched. Dec: Built as the *Empire Haig* for the Ministry of War Transport. Ellerman's Wilson Line as managers.
1946 July: Became *Dryden*, owned by Lamport & Holt.

1952 Transferred to Blue Star Line and renamed *Fremantle Star*.
1958 With her shift to the North Pacific coast run she was retitled *Catalina Star*.
1966 Reverted to Lamport & Holt to become *Devis*.
1969 Apr: Sold to Bry Overseas Navigation Inc, Panama; renamed *Mondia*.
1969 Dec 23: Arrived at Kaohsiung to be broken up by Han Tai Iron & Steel Co.

MALAY STAR

88 **MALAY STAR**
B 1952 Wm Pickersgill & Co, Sunderland. **T** 4,300g, 2,419n, 7,000 dwt.
D 410.6 (125.15) x 55.1 (16.79) x 24 (7.31).
E Sgl scr, oil, 6 cyls, 4S.SA. 12½ kts. By Harland & Wolff, Govan. Fuel 622 tons.
H Steel. 1 + shelter dk + part 3rd. **C** 362,525 cu ft (10,265 cu m) g.
1952 Feb: Ordered for the Booth S.S. Co as *Clement*. Transferred on the stocks to Blue Star ownership and launched Oct 4 as *Malay Star*. At this time the Austasia Line was in the process of formation and the naming system had not yet been finalised. In the event the suffix 'Star' was dropped. Feb: Entered service as *Malay*. The Austasia funnel design was adopted from the spot welded outline of the Blue Star funnel circle and star.
1953 March: Took Austasia's first sailing; it was from Singapore.
1964 Renamed *Mahsuri*.
1966 Transferred to Booth Line; r/n *Benedict*.
1967 Booth were giving all their main line vessels names commencing with 'R'. Renamed *Renoir*.
1971 Sold to Starlight Shippiung Co, S.A., Panama. R/n *Diamond Star*.
1973 Owned by Minlex Nav S.A.; same name. Starlight as managers. Oct 12: After lay up at Kaohsiung the vessel arrived at Suao, Taiwan for scrapping.

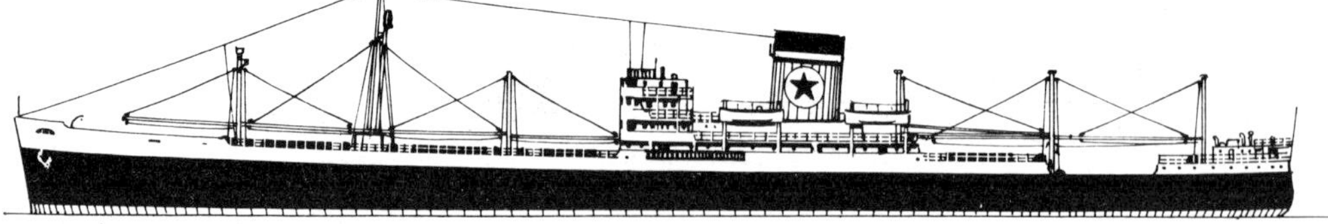

ENGLISH STAR, SCOTTISH STAR (II)

89 **ENGLISH STAR (I)**
B 1950 Fairfield S. B. & E. Co, Govan. **T** 9,996g, 5,950n, 12,992 dwt.
D 505.5 (154.08) oa, 484.5 (147.67) x 70.2 (21.4) x 35.9 (10.94).
E Tw scr, oil, 2 x 5 cyls 2 stroke dbl acting Doxford 11,600 BHP, 15½ kts. By builder.
H Steel. 2 dks + pt 3rd. F&B 392 (119.48). P 45 (13.72). **C** 637,000 cu ft (18,037.9 cu m) g. **P** 12.
1949 Dec 6: Launched for Blue Star Line.
1950 Oct: Delivered for employment on all routes; hence the non aligned name of the vessel.

1973 Sept 21: Arrived for breaking up by Chin Tai Steel Enterprise Co, Kaohsiung; work began in December.

90 **SCOTTISH STAR (II)**
Details as *English Star* (89) except: **T** 10,174g, 5,960n.
1950 May 15: Launched. Dec: Delivered.
1964 Transferred to Lamport & Holt. No other change.
1967 June 4: Joined a convoy for the northbound transit of the Suez Canal. June 5: Trapped together with 14 other ships in the Great Bitter Lake when the canal was blocked by scuttled Egyptian ships during the Arab-Israeli war. The ship's refrigeration plant kept the fruit in good condition.
1968 Egypt commenced to clear the canal but Israeli troops opened fire and the attempt was abandoned. After a period of 18 months *Scottish Star's* refrigeration plant was closed down because the deciduous fruit was rotting.
1970 The ship was abandoned, as the others also were, to the underwriters. Owned by Standard Steamship Owners Mutual War Risks Association, Scottish Star Ltd.
1975 May 30: Towed to Port Said. Sept 6: Arrived at Piraeus under the name of *Kavo Yerakas* for survey. Although outwardly the ship looked to be in fine shape her rotting fruit had eroded the hull and there was severe deterioration. Her cargo of wool was salved and sold by the new owners Defteron Corp, Piraeus. Laid up there and then sold for scrap.
1979 Broken up in Spain.

TRINIDAD STAR/ALBION STAR (II)/NORMAN STAR (II), BARFLEUR/ROMAN STAR (II)

91 **TRINIDAD STAR/ALBION STAR (II)/NORMAN STAR (II)**
B 1939 Burmeister & Wain, Copenhagen. **T** 3,022g, 1,785n.
D 336.3 (102.5) oa, 324.3 (98.85) x 45.8 (13.96) x 26.1 (7.95).
E Sgl scr, oil, 2 stroke sgl acting, 9 cyls, 12 kts. By builder. **H** Steel. 2 dks + pt 3rd.
1939 Oct: Built as *Mosdale* for A/S Mosvold Shipping Co, Norway.
1954 May: Sold to Blue Star Line Ltd with the intention of being renamed *Trinidad Star* for West Indies service in the banana trade but within days she was renamed *Albion Star* for the same service. Then was at once transferred to Lamport & Holt to become *Balzac*.
1959 Renamed *Carroll* by Lamport & Holt.
1960 Feb: Reverted to Blue Star as *Norman Star*. Converted at Middle Docks, South Shields, for the carriage of edible oils in tanks.
1961 Went across to Booth Line as *Basil*.
1964 May: Sold to H. & D. Kyriakos, owned by Eleni D. Kyprianou, and renamed *Eleni K*.
1966 Sold again, this time to Helen Shipping Corp, Panama Ltd, Greek flag, and called *Eleni Kypriakou*.
1969 Renamed *Olga*, same owners.
1970 Acquired by Kreta Shipping Co, S.A., new name *Georgios Markakis*.
1973 Sold to Amarinthis Shipping Co as *Nikos*. Broken up during the same year by Hierros Ardes, Bilbao.

92 BARFLEUR/ROMAN STAR (II)
Details as *Albion Star* except **B** 1938. **T** 3,000g, 1,759n. **D** 326.4 (98.94).
1938 Sept: Built as *Barfleur* for Compagnie Générale d'Armements Maritimes, Paris. West Indies fruit carrier, mainly bananas.
1947 Transferred to the parent company Cie Générale Transatlantique (French line). Same service.
1955 Sold to Blue Star Ltd as *Barfleur* but passed to Lamport & Holt as *Boswell* without bearing a '*Star*' name.
1960 Became *Crome*, same ownership. Mar: Transferred to Blue Star and renamed *Roman Star* at Liverpool. Converted at Middle Dock, South Shields for the carriage of edible oils in tanks. The refrigerated capacity being removed.
1961 May: Transferred; this time to Booth S.S. Co as *Bede*.
1964 Sold to Rahcassi Shipping Co; renamed *Victoria Elena*.
1967 Jan 16: Burnt out at Thessalonika to become a total loss. The ship was now acting as a general carrier because the fire broke out in a cargo of cotton. Sept: At La Spezia by Lotti S.p.A.

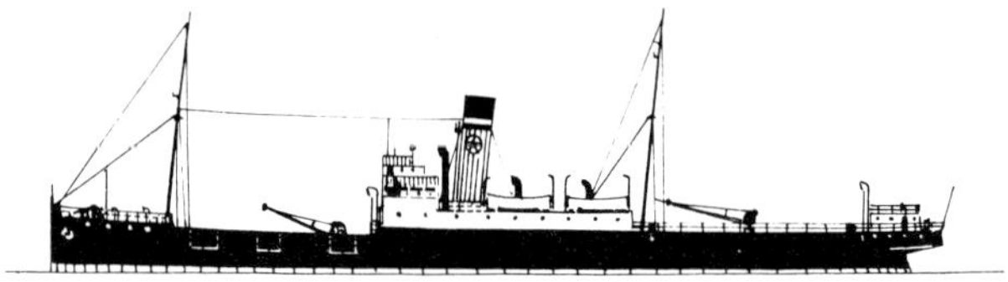

DROVER

93 **DROVER**
B 1923 Caledon S. B. & E. Co, Dundee. **T** 1,497g, 584n.
D 280.5 (85.5) oa, 270 (82.3) x 37.2 (11.34) x 17.4 (5.3).
E Sgl scr, tpl exp, 3 cyls, 2 sgl ended blrs Stm P: 185 lb. 10 kts. By builder.
1923 Aug: Completed as *Copeland* for Clyde S.S. Co. Based at Glasgow.
1946 Sold to G. Heyn & Sons, Head Line. Renamed *North Down*, North Continental Shipping Co.
1954 Oct: Acquired by Union International Co. Renamed *Drover*. After a month the ship was disposed of to Belfast S.S. Co and became *Ulster Herdsman*. Clearly there was nothing wrong with the ship because she gave sturdy service for over a decade of Irish Sea work.
1964 Broken up at Passage West, Cork, by Haulbowline Industries.

GEELONG STAR

94 **GEELONG STAR**
B 1945 Harland & Wolff, Belfast. **T** 8,641g, 6,197n, 10,595 dwt.
D 456 (139) oa, 439 (133.81) x 62.3 (18.99) x 33.9 (10.33).
E Sgl scr, oil, 6 cyls, 2 stroke dbl acting. 13 kts. By builder. Fuel 907 tons.
H Steel. 3 dks. F 32 (9.75) B 181 (55.17). C 669,000 cu ft (18,944 cu m)g.
1945 Feb 28: Launched as *Defoe* for Lamport & Holt. May: Delivered. This was the last of the

five 'D' class and the only one with a long bridgedeck on the standard design hull.
1954 Apr: Transferred to Blue Star and renamed *Geelong Star*. Refrigeration was installed by the builder.
1958 Apr: Reverted to Lamport & Holt and *Defoe*.
1966 Feb: Sold to Astrofeliz Cia Nav S.A. Renamed *Argolis Star*. Later Argolis Shipping Co.
1969 Oct 17: Left Singapore for breaking up. Oct 29: Arrived for breaking up at Shanghai.

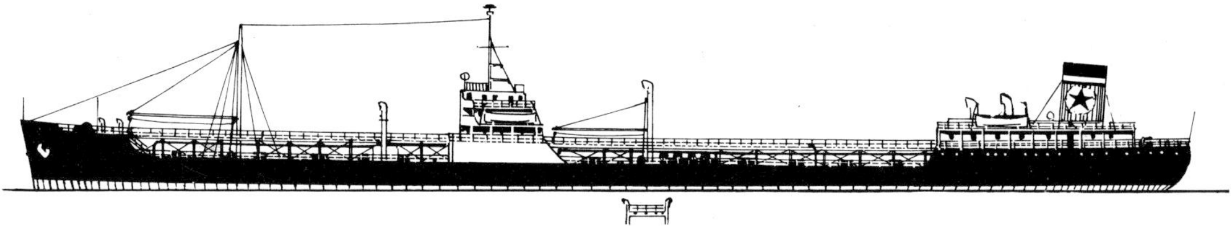

PACIFIC STAR (III)

95 **PACIFIC STAR (III)**
B 1954 Wm Hamilton & Co Ltd, Port Glasgow. **T** 11,218g, 6,328n, 16,700 dwt.
D 546 (166.42) oa, 521.4 (158.92) x 69.3 (21.12) x 38.6 (11.77).
E Sgl scr, oil, 5 cyls, 2 stroke sgl acting, Doxford type, 13 kts. By D. Rowan & Co, Glasgow. Fuel 1,378 tons at 19 tons per day. **H** Steel. 1 dk. **F** 50 (15.24). **B** 48 (14.63). **P** 118 (35.97). **C** 804,362 cu ft (22,777 cu m) oil in 27 tanks, 9 centre, 9 port and 9 starboard.
1954 Jan 22: Launched. April: Complered as Blue Star's only oil tanker. Owned by Booth S.S. Co on bare-boat charter to Blue Star.
1961 Apr: Transferred to Blue Star ownership. Because of the Suez Canal closure and the building of very large tankers *Pacific Star* became uneconomical in the spot market.
1964 Sept: Sold for £160,000 to Atlantic Overseas Bulk Carriers; renamed *Silver Bay*.
1973 Apr 22: Arrived at Kaohsiung for demolition by Jung Ho Steel Enterprises.

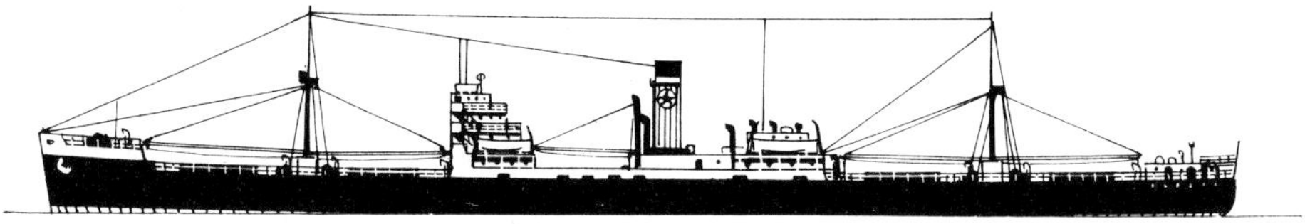

OREGON STAR (IV)

96 **OREGON STAR (IV)**
B 1943 Lithgow's Ltd, Port Glasgow. **T** 7,040g, 4,973n, 9,740 dwt.
D 447.6 (136.43) oa, 432.7 (131.89) x 56.2 (17.13) x 34.2 (10.42).
E Sgl scr, tpl exp, 3 cyls, 558 NHP, 2 sgl ended blrs, Stm P: 220 lb, 10½ kts.
By J. G. Kincaid, Greenock. Fuel 1,251 tons.
H Steel. 2 dks. **F** 39 (11.89) **C** 426,500 cu ft (12,077.2 cu m) bale.
1942 Dec 28: Launched.
1943 Mar: Delivered as *Empire Treasure*, Ministry of War Transport, Port Line as managers.
1946 May: Sold to Donaldson Line. Renamed *Gracia*. Served on the Pacific coast of North America route with occasional summer voyages to Hudson's Bay.

1954 Acquired by Blue Star together with the Donaldson assets, ships and rights to the Pacific coast service. Renamed *Oregon Star*.
1955 May: Sold to Williamson & Co, Hong Kong. Renamed *Inchleana*.
1966 March: Became *Tetulia* of the National Shipping Corporation of Pakistan.
1969 Broken up at Gadani Beach, Karachi, by Mohamadi Iron Traders.

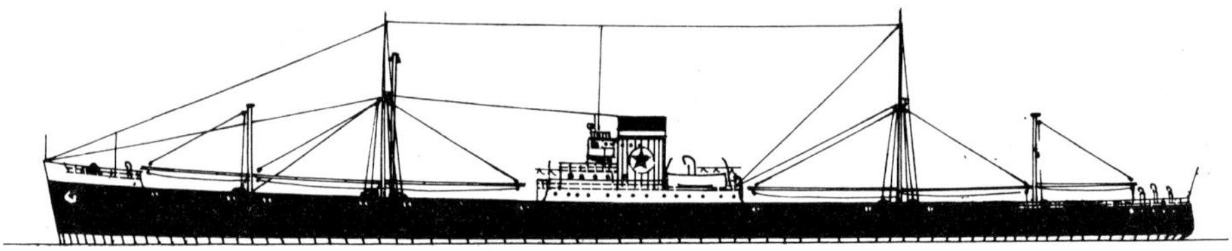

PORTLAND STAR, SEATTLE STAR, OAKLAND STAR (I)

97 **PORTLAND STAR**
B 1937 Harland & Wolff, Belfast. **T** 7,783g, 4,865n, 10,470 dwt.
D 456 (139) oa, 438.6 (133.69) x 62.3 (18.99) x 25.4 (7.74).
E Sgl scr, oil, 2 stroke dbl acting, 6 cyls, 12 kts. By builder. Fuel 902 tons.
H Steel. 3 dks. F 32 (9.75) B 83 (25.3) C 590,000 cu ft (16,707 cu m)g.
1937 Apr 12: Launched. July: Completed for Lamport & Holt as *Delius*. The first of three general cargo vessels with a revolutionary design to the superstructure; the bridge and funnel being amalgamated. Two later ships, with the same hull design, took the mode even further.
1940 Apr 27: Suffered damage by air attack, at Romdalsfjord during the Norwegian campaign.
1943 Nov 21: Attacked and damaged by torpedo carrying aircraft of S.W. Ireland but made port safely.
1954 Transferred to Blue Star Line as *Portland Star*. Placed on the ex-Donaldson north Pacific coast of North America service.
1958 Reverted to *Delius*, Lamport & Holt, when removed from the Pacific run.
1961 Oct: Sold to Compagnie Metallurgique et Miniere S.A., Casablanca, for sale to shipbreakers. Renamed *Kettara VII*. Oct 28: Left Hull for Casablanca where she loaded a final cargo of scrap metal for Japan. The ship was then broken up by Izumi-Ohtsu.

98 **SEATTLE STAR**
Details as *Portland Star* (97) except: **B** 1938. **T** 7,761g, 4,854n, 10,469 dwt.
1937 Oct 21: Launched.
1938 Jan: Completed as *Delane* for Lamport & Holt. The speed of these three ships was less than some of their older contemporaries but they were regarded as extremely economical and 'fast enough'.
1954 Transferred to Blue Star Line and renamed *Seattle Star* for the Pacific route. All three of the transferred ships were sent to the builder to have refrigerated plant installed.
1961 June: Sold for eventual scrapping to Cie Metallurgique et Miniere S.A., Casablanca. Renamed *Kettara VI*. July 15: Sailed from Casablanca with scrap for Osaka. Oct: Delivered to Hong Kong for breaking up by Hong Kong Rolling Mills.

99 **OAKLAND STAR (I)**
Details as *Portland Star* (97) except: **B** 1944. **T** 8,148g, 5,831n, 9,972 dwt.
D 456.3 (139.08) oa, 439 (133.81). Fuel 857 tons.
H 3 dks + pt 4th. F 38 (17.68). B 71 (21.64).
1944 Mar 23: Launched. Aug: Completed as *Devis* for Lamport & Holt.

1955 Transferred to Blue Star Management for the North Pacific service. Renamed *Oakland Star*. Refrigeration installed by builder.
1957 Reverted to Lamport & Holt and *Devis*.
1962 July 4: Arrived at Spezia for scrapping by Cantieri Navali del Golfo, La Spezia.

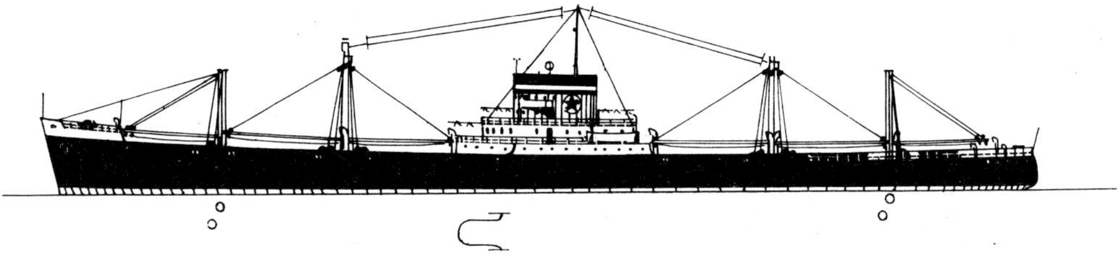

WASHINGTON STAR

100 **WASHINGTON STAR**
B 1940 Harland & Wolff, Belfast. **T** 8,105g, 5,858n, 10,090 dwt.
D 456 (138.99) oa, 438.8 (133.75) x 62.3 (18.99) x 33.9 (10.33).
E Sgl scr, oil, 6 cyls, 2 stroke dbl acting. 13 kts. By builder. Fuel 860 tons.
H Steel. 3 dks + pt 4th. F 33 (10.06). B 71 (21.64). C 526,000 cu ft (14,894.7 cu m)g.
1940 May: Built as *Debrett* for Lamport & Holt; general cargo vessel.
1955 July: Passed to Blue Star Line and renamed *Washington Star*, the state not the capital of the U.S.A., for the North Pacific coast route.
1956 Reverted to *Debrett*.
1964 Sold to Embajada Cia Nav S.A., renamed *Ambasciata*. This concern was one of a few who specialised in buying ships, loading them with one ad hoc cargo, delivering this to a Far East destination at a minimum price and then disposed of the ship for scrap. Astroguarda and Metallurgique are two other examples. Dec 28: Arrived at Osaka for breaking up.

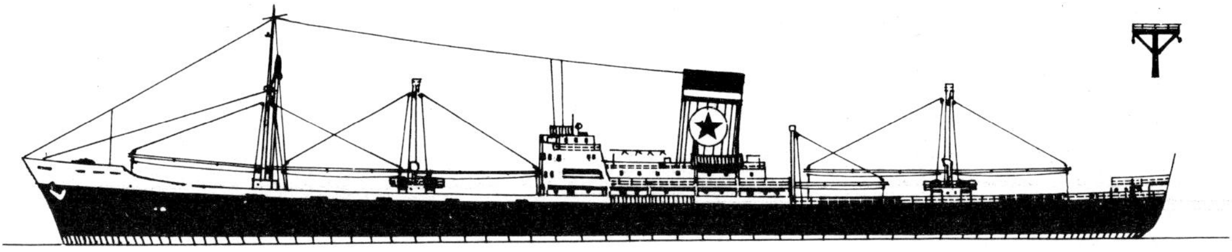

CANBERRA STAR/BUENOS AIRES STAR (II), NEWCASTLE STAR/MONTEVIDEO STAR, HOBART STAR/BUENOS AIRES STAR (I)/HOBART STAR

101 **CANBERRA STAR/BUENOS AIRES STAR (II)**
B 1956 Bremer Vulkan Schiffsbau und Maschinenfabrik, Bremen-Vegesack.
T 8,257g, 4,966n, 12,345 dwt. **D** 519.5 (158.35) oa 470 (143.26) x 70.3 (21.43) x 30 (9.14).
E Sgl scr, oil, 10 cyls M.A.N., 2 stroke sgl acting, 11,250 BHP, 17½ kts. Fuel 1,770 tons. By builder.
H Steel. 2 dks + pt 4th. F 52.2 (15.9). 5 hatches. C 325,988 cu ft (9,231 cu m) refrig. Cools to -18°C. Derricks 1 x 50 ton installed.
1956 Dec 25: Launched. May: Delivered. Owned by Salient Shipping Co (Bermuda) Ltd, Hamilton, Bermuda. U.K.—Australia—New Zealand service. The first of the five foreign built ships which

were the cause of much comment at the time. Blue Star had been known for their 'build in Britain' policy until now.
1973 Jan: Renamed *Buenos Aires Star* to replace *Hobart Star* (103) which had been transferred to the South American route but following collision damage had been withdrawn and reverted to her original name.
1979 Dec 27: Broken up by Lung Fa Steel & Iron Co Ltd, Kaohsiung.

102 NEWCASTLE STAR/MONTEVIDEO STAR
Details as *Canberra Star* (101) except: **T** 8,398g, 4,934n, 12,150 dwt.
H C 397,030 cu ft (11,242.7 cu m)g. As a refrigerated ship the capacity was a little less at 326,000 cu ft (9,231.3 cu m).
1956 May 28: Launched. Oct: Delivered to Blue Star Line Ltd as registered at London.
1973 Renamed *Montevideo Star*. With *Canberra Star* these two ships acted as non-passenger replacements for the three passenger ships which were now being broken up in Taiwan. *Queensland Star* was the third.
1975 Laid up at Barry Dock. Now uner Blue Star Ship Management Co.
1976 Sold to Conquest Shipping Co, Limassol. R/n *Golden Madonna*.
1978 Owned by Universe Sunset Marine Inc, Piraeus; same name.
1980 Mar 13: Arrived for breaking up by Gi Yuen Steel Enterprise Co, Kaohsiung.

103 **HOBART STAR/BUENOS AIRES STAR (I)/HOBART STAR**
Details as *Canberra Star* (101) except: **T** 8,257g, 4,937n, 12,162 dwt.
1956 July: Built for Salient Shipping Co (Bermuda) Ltd, Bermudian flag.
1962 British flag.
1972 Transferred to the South American service; renamed *Buenos Aires Star*. Nov: After only one voyage bearing her new name the ship was damaged by collision and was replaced by *Canberra Star*. Reverted to *Hobart Star*.
1978 Sold to Atacos Cia Nav S.A. (Enais Shipping Co managers). Greek flag. Renamed *Aegean Prosperity*. Controlled by Fairmont Shipping Co S.A., Panama.
1980 Mar 28: Broken up by An Hsiung Iron & Steel Co, Kaohsiung.

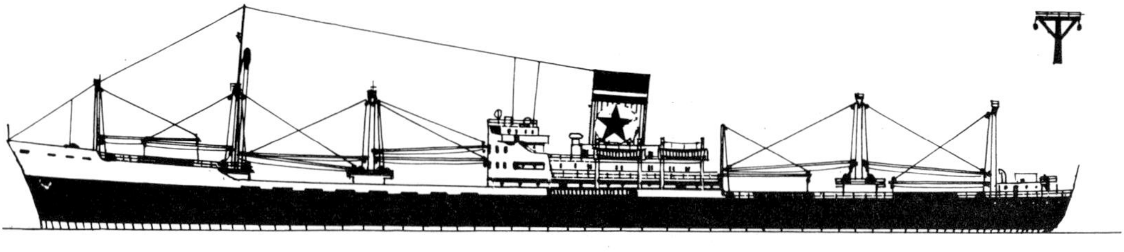

GLADSTONE STAR, TOWNSVILLE STAR

104 **GLADSTONE STAR**
B 1957 Bremer Vulkan S.u.M., Bremen-Vegesack. **T** 10,635g, 6,432n, 12,253 dwt.
D 516.3 (157.38) oa, 470 (143.21) x 70.3 (21.42) x 30.4 (9.27).
E Sgl scr, oil, 10 cyls, 2 stroke sgl acting, 11,250 BHP, 17 kts. By builder.
H Steel. 2 dks + pt 3rd. F 100 (30.5). 5 hatches. C 410,000 cu ft (11,610 cu m) refrig.
1957 May 28: Launched. Oct: Delivered to Salient Shipping Co (Bermuda) Ltd, Hamilton, with Blue Star Line Ltd as managers. Australian service.
1958 Transferred to the British registry and flag.
1982 Sold to Kate Shipping Co, Malta. R/n *Gladys*. Oct 16: Arrived at Gadani Beach for breaking up by United Steel Scrapping Mills.

105 **TOWNSVILLE STAR**
Details as 104 except: **T** 10,632g, 6,432n, 12,353 dwt.
1057 Aug 22: Launched. Dec: Delivered to Salient Shipping Co (Bermuda) Ltd with Blue Star as managers. Australian routes.
1958 Transferred to London registry.
1962 Aug 25: Left Brisbane on the first sailing of the new Australia—East Coast of U.S.A. and Canada service. Made three round trips per annum.
1978 Dec 15: Trapped for two months at Khorramshahr by the Iraq-Iran war.
1980 Her final voyage was with 160,000 carcases of meat Australia—Odessa. July 14: Arrived at Kaohsiung for breaking up by Nan Long Steel & Iron Co.

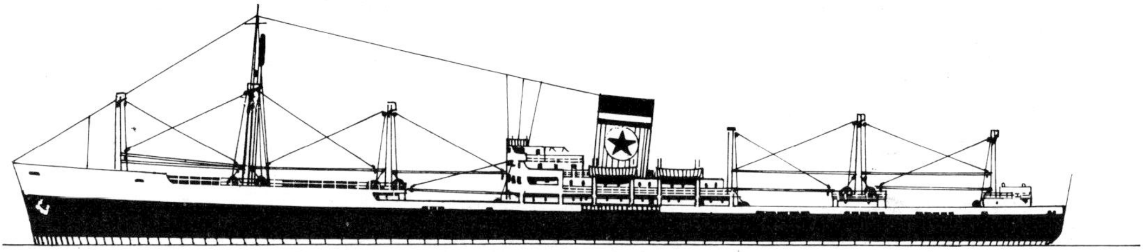

QUEENSLAND STAR/BRASILIA STAR

106 **QUEENSLAND STAR/BRASILIA STAR**
B 1957 Fairfield S. B. & E. Co, Govan. **T** 9,920g, 6,422n, 11,000 dwt.
D 511.5 (155.91) oa, 471 (143.56) x 68.3 (20.82) x 30.1 (9.17).
E Sgl scr, oil, 2 x 5 cyls Doxford, 2 stroke sgl acting, 11,600 BHP, 17 kts. By builder.
H Steel. 2 dks + pt 3rd and 4th. F 175 (53.34). 5 hatches. C 389,000 cu ft (11,015.3 cu m) refrig. Derrick 1 x 50 ton.
1957 March 15: Launched as *Queensland Star* for Blue Star Line Ltd. Nov: Delivered.
1964 Transferred to Lamport & Holt ownership; remained on bare-boat charter to Blue Star.
1965 Reverted to Blue Star ownership.
1972 Aug: Renamed *Brasilia Star* for the South American route where she acted as one of the four replacement ships for the passenger vessels.
1975 Managed by Blue Star Ship Management (BSSM).
1979 Nov 16: Left Newhaven, Sussex, for breaking up.
1980 Jan 14: Arrived at Kaohsiung for demolition by Lung Fa Steel & Iron Co.

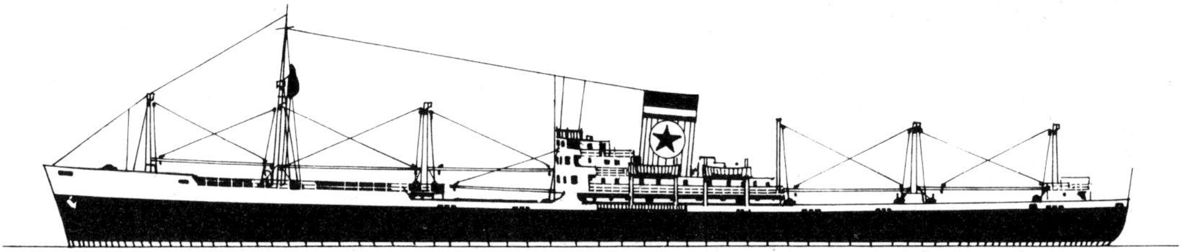

ROCKHAMPTON STAR

107 **ROCKHAMPTON STAR**
Sister to *Queensland Star* (106) except: **B** 1958 Cammell Laird & Co (S. B. & E.) Ltd, Birkenhead. **T** 10,619g, 6,407n, 9,600 dwt.

D 507.1 (154.59) oa, 470 (143.26)bp.
E 8 cyls, 13,300 BHP Harland & Wolff-Burmeister & Wain type, 107 rpm, 17½ kts. By builder.
H F 172 (52.43). C 417,827 cu ft (11,831.6 cu m), 2/3 refrigerated and 1/3 chilled.
Derricks 1 x 50 ton, 8 x 3 ton, 6 x 5 ton, 4 x 10 ton, 2 x 15 ton.
1957 Sept 24: Launched for Blue Star Line.
1958 Jan: Completed. April: Maiden sailing London—Northern Australian ports.
1964 Transferred to Lamport & Holt but remained on bare-boat charter to Blue Star.
1965 Reverted to Blue Star Line Ltd ownership.
1975 Managed by Blue Star Ship Management.
1981 Laid up at Falmouth. Sold to Festasi Shipping Co S.A., Panama. R/n *Golden Lady*.
1982 May: Sold for breaking up at Karachi. Resold to Bangladesh.
1983 June 20: Arrived at Chittagong and scrapped there.

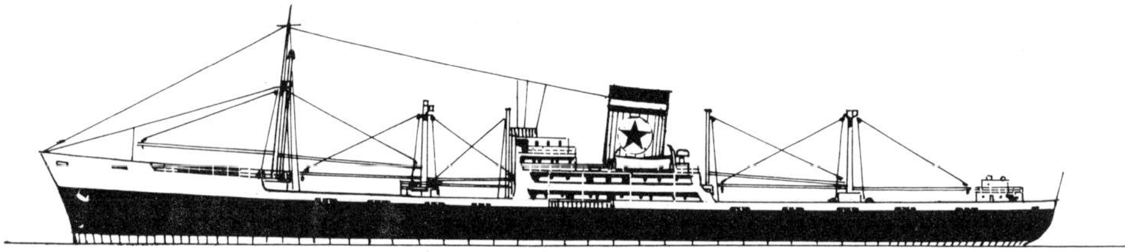

CANADIAN STAR (II)

108 **CANADIAN STAR (II)**
B 1957 Caledon S. B. & E. Co, Dundee. **T** 6,291g, 3,639n, 9,185 dwt.
D 473.3 (144.26)bp x 63.3 (19.29) x 28 (8.53) main deck, 39.5 (12.04) shelter deck closed.
E Sgl scr, oil, 6 cyls, 2 stroke sgl acting, Scott-Doxford type, 8,000 BHP, 16 kts.
By Scotts S. B. & E. Co, Greenock.
H Steel. 1 dk + shelter dk. F 95 (28.96). 5 holds. C 567,890 cu ft (16080.1 cu m)ins.
Derrick 10 x 5 ton, 6 x 10 ton, 1 x 50 ton. **P** 12.
1956 Oct 5: Launched; Blue Star Line Ltd.
1957 Feb: Completed. The forecastle carried general cargo; the remainder of the space was refrigerated. Two moulded depths are shown to indicate the difference in the dimension when the vessel is operating either as an open or a closed shelter decker.
1967 Converted by Cammell Lairds to carry containers as well as normal cargo.
1972 Passed to Lamport & Holt on bare-boat charter. Renamed *Raeburn*.
1979 Sold to Vertigo Shipping Co Ltd, Limassol; r/n *Braeburn*, Panamanian flag. Mar 1: Left Casablanca for Taiwan owned by Ahmed Lines, Panama. May 9: Arrived for demolition by Keun Hwa Iron & Steel Works.

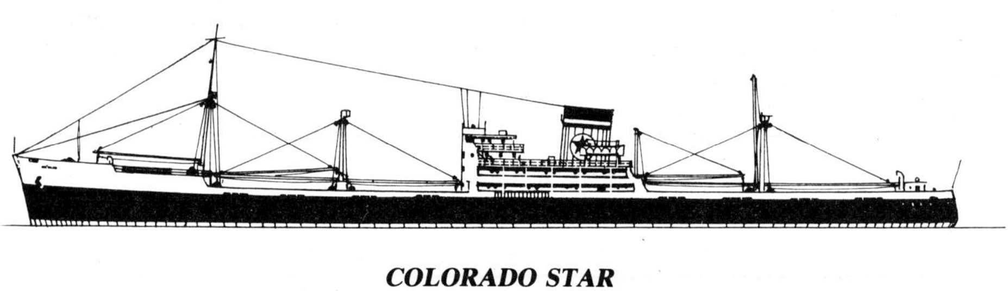

COLORADO STAR

109 **COLORADO STAR**
B 1952 Harland & Wolff, Belfast. **T** 8,292g, 4,968n, 10,488 dwt.
D 466 (142.04) oa x 63.4 (19.32) x 28.8 (8.78).
E Sgl scr, oil, 7 cyls, 2 stroke sgl acting, B&W type, 16 kts. By builder.
H Steel. 2 dks + pt 3rd. F 94 (28.65). C 568,000 cu ft (16,084.1 cu m) refrig.
1952 Aug 6: Launched. Nov: Delivered as *Raeburn* for Lamport & Holt.
1958 Transferred to Blue Star on bare-boat charter. Renamed *Colorado Star*.
1972 Reverted to Lamport & Holt; re-chartered to Austasia Line; renamed *Mahsuri* (I).
1977 Renamed *Roland* upon reversion to Lamport & Holt. Never Blue Star owned.
1978 Oct 5: Arrived at Faslane for breaking up by Shipbreaking Industries Ltd.

110 **SIDDONS**
B 1959 George Brown & Co (Marine) Ltd, Greenock. **T** 1,282g, 566n . **D** 265.3 (88.86) oa x 41.9 (12.75) x 15.1 (4.6).
E Sgl scr, oil, 8 cyls, 4 stroke sgl acting, 2000 BHP, 12 kts. By M. A. N. Hamburg.
H Steel. 1 dk + shelter dk. F 30 (9.14) B 60 (18.29).
1959 Apr: Laid down for Blue Star Line Ltd but completed as *Siddons* for the group's Lamport & Holt services. This ship never served with Blue Star and is included for record purposes only.

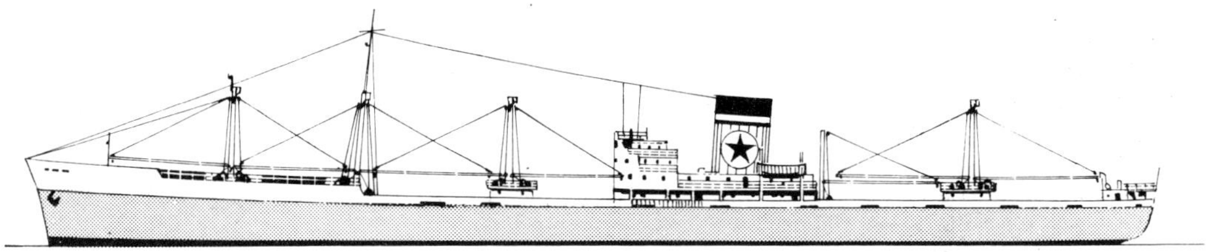

ULSTER STAR

111 **ULSTER STAR**
B 1959 Harland & Wolff, Belfast. **T** 10,413g, 6,341n, 9,900 dwt.
D 519.3 (158.28) oa, 490 (149.35) x 70.4 (21.46) x 27.6 (8.41).
E Sgl scr, oil, 6 cyls, 2 stroke sgl acting, 10,000 BHP, B&W type, 17 kts. By builder.
H Steel. 2 dks + pt 3rd. F 153 (46.63). 6 hatches. C 436,820 cu ft (12,369.4 cu m) refrig. Derricks 2 x 10 ton, 8 x 5 ton, 10 x 3 ton.
1959 Feb 26: Launched. July: Trials. Placed on Australian service.
1964 Transferred to Lamport & Holt ownership bare-boat chartered to Blue Star.
1965 Reverted to Blue Star ownership.
1972 *Ulster Star* was the fourth ship to be transferred to the South American route when the passenger ships were withdrawn. Because her assignment was not necessarily long term she became the one ship whose name was not changed.
1975 Managed by BSSM.
1979 Oct 3: At Kaohsiung for scrapping by Nan Hor Steel Enterprises Co.

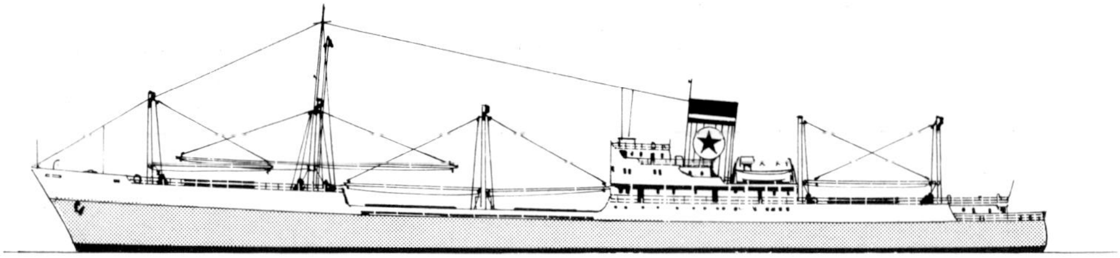

A. CANTERBURY STAR (I), MONTREAL STAR/AMERICA STAR

112 **CANTERBURY STAR (I)**
B 1960 Bartram & Sons, Sunderland. **T** 7,539g, 4,140n, 9,400 dwt.
D 462.8 (141.06) oa, 425 (129.54) x 63.2 (19.26) x 30.1 (9.17).
E Sgl scr, oil, 2 stroke sgl acting, 8 cyls, Sulzer 8RD 76 type, 12,000 BHP, 17 kts.
By G. Clark & Co, Sunderland.
H Steel. 2 dks + pt 3rd. F 128 (29.01). B 160 (48.77). 4 hatches.
C 349,600 cu ft (9,900 cu m) ins; 98,200 cu ft (2,780.7 cu m) general.
1960 June 9: Launched. Dec: Delivered to Union International with Blue Star as managers. The first of a class of five ships of which the last pair had deck cranes (of differing design) in place of pole masts and king posts.
1963 Ownership became Blue Star Line Ltd.
1975 Managed by Blue Star Ship Management (BSSM).
1980 July 11: Arrived at Bombay for breaking up by Ghaziran Gokulchand & Co at their Darukhana berth.

113 **MONTREAL STAR**
Sister to *Canterbury Star* (112) except: **B** 1963. **T** 7,365g, 4,186n, 9,400 dwt.
D 462.9 (141.09) oa, 424.1 (129.26)bp. **H** F 121 (36.88). B 158 (48.16).
1962 Dec 14: Launched for Blue Star Line Ltd.
1963 Sept: Entered service on the Australia—East coast U.S.A. and Canada route joining *Townsville Star* which had inaugurated the service in the previous year.
1975 Managed by BSSM.
1980 Aug 1: Arrived at Gadani Beach. Sept: Scrapped by Noori Trading Corp.

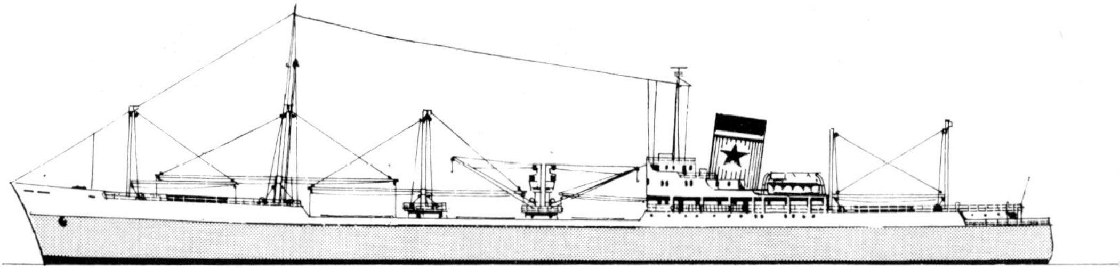

B. AMERICA STAR

114 **AMERICA STAR**
Sister of *Canterbury Star* (112) except: **B** 1963. **T** 7,365g, 4,186n, 9,400 dwt.
D & **H** as *Montreal Star*.
1963 Aug 19: Launched.

1964 Jan: Entered service on the Australia—U.S.A.—Canada east coast route.
1972 Nov: Lengthened by 78ft (23.77m) at Framnaes yard, Sandfjord, Norway (Drawing 114B). **D** 540 4 (164.71). **T** 9,253g, 11,700 dwt. Refrigeration adapted for the carriage of bananas which require special temperature control to prevent them ripening before the delivery to shops process.
1973 April 4: Resumed service. Sailed for Cape Town.
1975 Managed by BSSM.
1982 Sold at Avonmouth to Vermerar Cia Nav, Panama. R/n *Golden Princess*.
1984 June: Broken up at Shanghai.

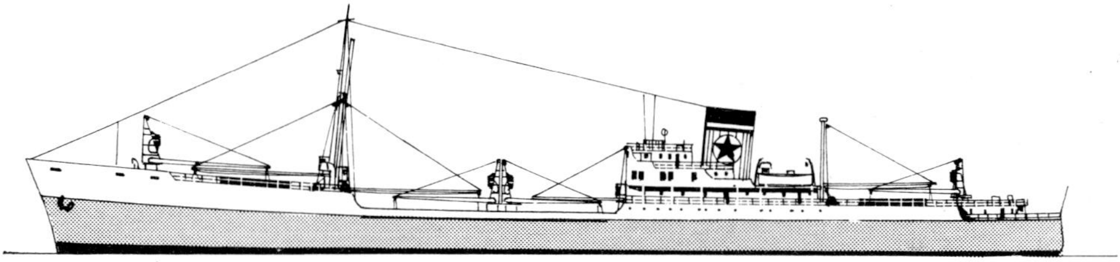

QUEBEC STAR/HALIFAX STAR

115 **QUEBEC STAR/HALIFAX STAR**
Details as *Canterbury Star* (112) except: **B** 1964. **T** 7,327g, 4,199n, 9,294 dwt.
D 462.9 (141.09) oa, 424.1 (129.26)bp. **H** B 172 (52.43). 4 deck cranes replaced three stump masts.
1964 Jan 29: Launched as *Halifax Star*. The vessel had been intended to carry the name *Quebec Star* but was changed when the ships were classed as having the names of the major ports of call on the route.
1972 July: Lengthened at Sandfjord similarly to her sisters. **T** 9,220g.
1975 To Blue Star Ship Management.
1983 Laid up at the River Fal. Oct: Sold for breaking up in China. Final voyage Taichung—Beilun.

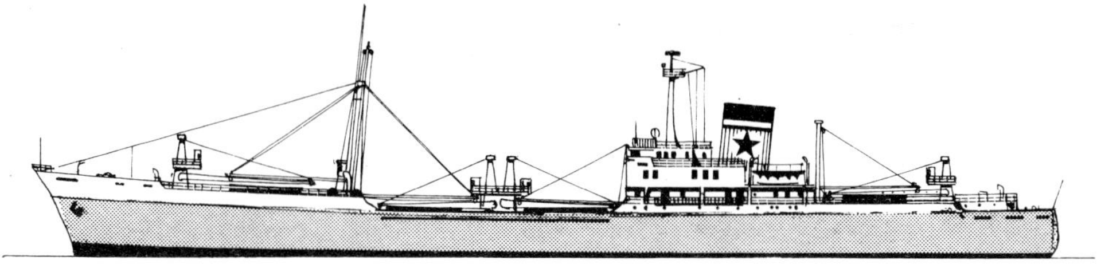

NEW YORK STAR

116 **NEW YORK STAR**
Details as *Canterbury Star* (112) except: **B** 1965. **T** 7,372g, 4,161n, 9,403 dwt.
D As *Montreal Star*. **E** By G. Clark & N. E. M. Ltd. **H** F 121 (36.88) Deck cranes.
1965 Feb 3: Launched. Sept: Commissioned for Blue Star Line.
1972/3 Lengthened at Sandfjord as *America Star*.
1975 BSSM management.
1980 Transferred to the Italian subsidiary Calmedia S.p.A. di Nav, Panama. Managed by Blue Star Ship Management. R/n *Liguria*.
1981 Sold to Panama Shipping Co. Same managers.
1983 Sold to Euroatlantic Shipping Corp for her loaded delivery voyage to the breakers. Dec: Arrive at Gadani Beach; scrapped by Ahmed Mercantile.

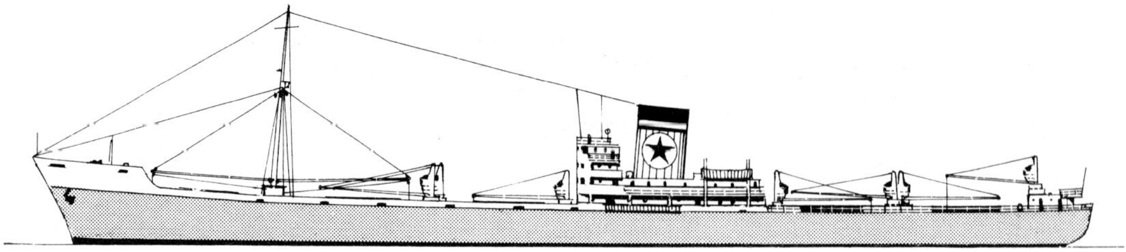

FREMANTLE STAR (II)

117 **FREMANTLE STAR (II)**
B 1960 Cammell Laird & Co (S. B. & Eng) Ltd, Birkenhead. **T** 8,403g, 4,949n, 12,171 dwt.
D 519 (158.19) oa, 470 (143.26) x 70.2 (21.4) x 30 (9.14).
E Sgl scr, oil, 8 cyls, 2 stroke sgl acting, 13,300 BHP, 18 kts. By Harland & Wolff, Belfast.
H Steel. 1 dk + shelter dk + pt 3rd and 4th. **F** 53 (16.15). **C** 332,000 cu ft (9,401.2 cu m) refrig.
1959 Dec 30: Launched for Blue Star Line Ltd.
1960 Apr 27: Trials. May: Placed on the U.K.—Australia—New Zealand service.
1964 Transferred to Lamport & Holt; route and colours unchanged.
1965 Reverted to Blue Star Line ownership.
1975 Operated by Blue Star Ship Management.
1979 Renamed *Catarina* at Singapore by Caxton Marine Enterprises Corp.
1980 Jan 4: Demolition began by Nan Long Steel & Iron Co, Kaohsiung.

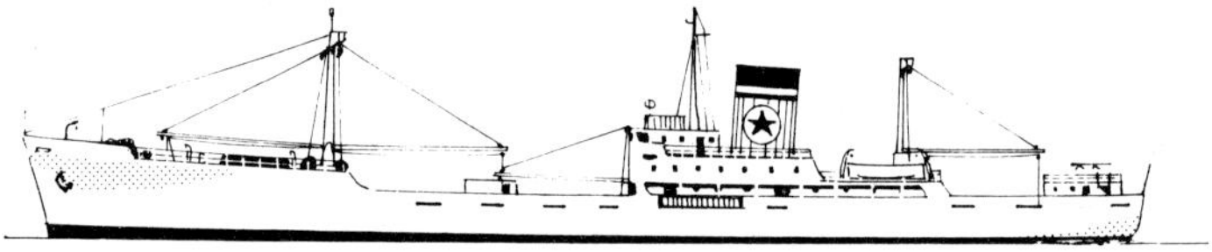

A. SANTOS STAR (I), MENDOZA STAR

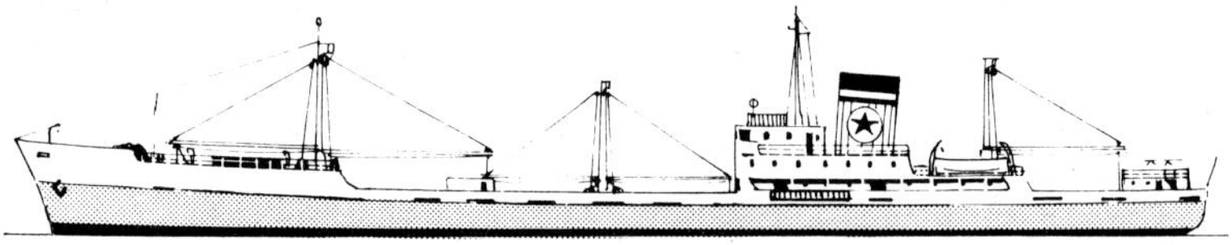

B. SANTOS STAR (I), MENDOZA STAR

118 **SANTOS STAR (I)**
B 1959 Brooke Marine Ltd, Lowestoft. **T** 3,594g, 1,999n, 3,751 dwt.
D 338 (103.02) oa, 310 (94.49) x 47.1 (14.36) x 20 (6.1).
E Sgl scr, oil, 7 cyls, 2 stroke sgl acting, 4,600 BHP, 16 kts. By M. A. N, Hamburg.
H Steel. 2 dks + pt 3rd. **F** 93 (28.35). **C** 174,263 cu ft (4,934 cu m)ins. 8 derricks.
1959 Dec: Completed as *Constable* for Lamport & Holt (Drawing A).
1962 Transferred to Blue Star Line; renamed *Santos Star*. Placed on the new service between South American ports and Italian and French Mediterranean terminals.
1964 Lengthened at Belfast by Harland & Wolff. **D** 391.5ft (119.33m) oa, **T** 3,775g (Drawing B).
1966 Transferred to Calmedia S.p.A. di Nav Cagliari; renamed *Calagaribaldi*.
1981 Became *Gafredo*; Nourfo Cia Naviera S.A., Panama.
1984 Apr 29: Arrived Bilbao for scrapping by Desguaces Maritimos S.A.

119 **MENDOZA STAR**
Details as *Santos Star* (118) except: **B** 1960 Alex Stephen & Sons, Linthouse.
T 3,563g, 1,972n, 3,553 dwt. **E** 5000 BHP Sulzer design. By builder.
1959 Dec 1: Launched.
1960 Feb: Completed as *Chatham* for Lamport & Holt.
1962 Apr: Transferred to Blue Star as *Mendoza Star*. Joined her sister on the South America—Italy service.
1963 Lengthened at Hoboken by S. A. Cockerill-Ougree similarly to *Santos Star*. **T** 3,666g.
1966 During the seamen's strike she was laid up in the River Blackwater.
1967 R/n *Calavittoria*, Calmedia S.p.A, di Nav, Cagliari, Sicily.
1979 Became *Briso Aegean*, Laguna Shipping Co; managers Laskaridis Shipping Ltd, Piraeus.
1980 Owned by Enias Shipping Co, Piraeus and then by Tobermory Shipping Co still with the same managers.
1984 March 23: Arrived at Gadani Beach for scrapping by Habib Maritime.

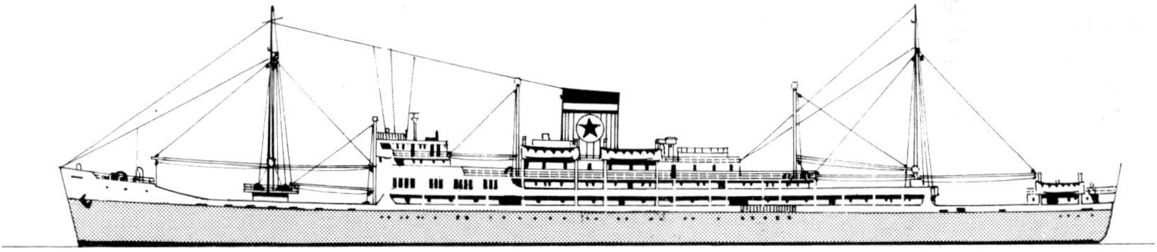

IBERIA STAR

120 **IBERIA STAR**
B 1950 John Cockerill S. A., Hoboken, Belgium. **T** 10,854g, 6,190n.
D 505 (153.92) oa, 468.5 (142.8) x 64.8 (19.75) x 27.5 (8.38).
E Sgl scr, oil, 8 cyls, 2 stroke dbl acting, 9,250 BHP, 16 kts. By builder at their Seraing works.
H Steel. 2 dks + pt 3rd. F 45 (13.72) 6 hatches.
C 172,231 cu ft (4,877 cu m)ins and 475,113 cu ft (13,453.7 cu m)g. **P** 98 1st, 200 2nd.
1950 Mar 3: Launched. Sept: Built as *Baudouinville* for Cie Maritime Belge. West Africa service.
1957 Renamed *Thysville*, same owner, due to the advent of a new *Baudouinville*.
1961 Feb: Sold to the Booth S.S. Co; renamed *Anselm*; Liverpool—Manaus route.
1963 Transferred to Blue Star Line Ltd; renamed *Iberia Star*. Converted for the carriage of chilled meat by Bremer Vulkan at Vegesack. **P** 248 1st. Placed on the Liverpool—River Plate service; later out of London.
1965 Chartered to the new Austasia Line Ltd; renamed *Australasia*. Blue Star Line continued as the owners.
1971 Registered in Singapore with Austasia as the owners; continued on the Australia—Far East service.
1972 Dec 16: Left Singapore in tow for breaking up. Her purchaser, Euroasia Carriers, were recorded as British.
1973 March: Broken up at Hualien by Chou's Iron & Steel (Industrial) Co.

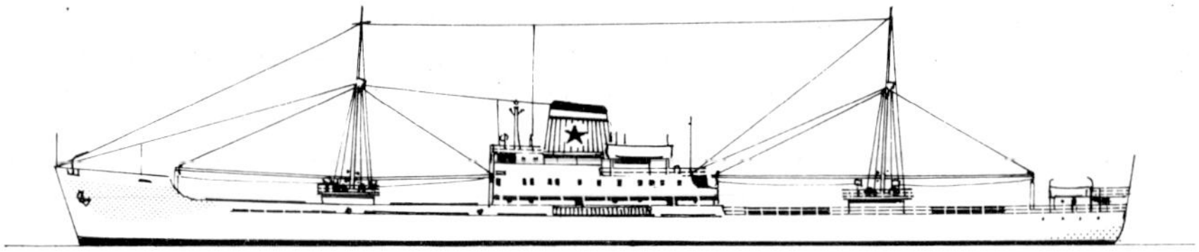

GENOVA STAR

121 **GENOVA STAR**
B 1956 Eriksbergs M/V A/B, Gothenburg. **T** 5,137g, 2,869n, 4,200 dwt.
D 396.5 (120.85) oa, 365 (111.25) x 54.1 (16.49) x 23.5 (7.16).
E Sgl scr, oil, 8 cyls, 2 stroke sgl acting, 5,700 BHP, B&W type, 15 kts. By builder.
H Steel. 4 dks. 4 hatches. C 207,100 cu ft (5,864.4 cu m)ins for the carriage of bananas and deciduous fruit.
1956 Aug 24: Launched as *Norefjell* for Olsen & Ugelstad.
1964 Acquired by Blue Star and renamed *Genova Star* for their South America—Italy service.
1966 Transferred to Calmedia S.p.A. di Nav; renamed *Calabella*; same service.
1974 Became *Annaflora*, Nouro Cia Nav S.A., Piraeus.
1978 Renamed *Nissos Samos*, Samos Shipping Enterprises, Piraeus.
1981 June 21: At Gadani Beach for breaking up by Paruma (Eastern) Ltd.

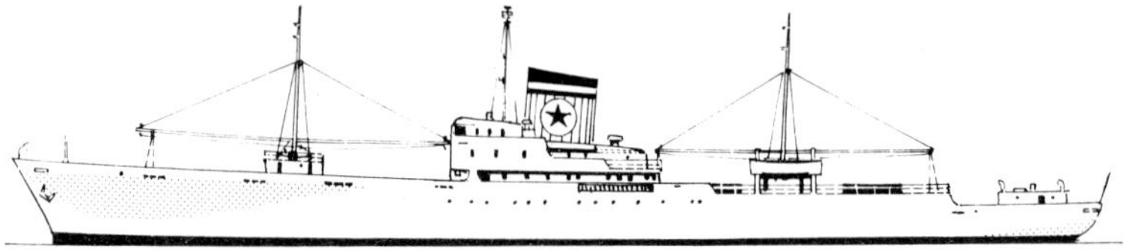

PADOVA STAR, BARCELONA STAR

122 **PADOVA STAR**
B 1956 Deutsches Werft, Hamburg. **T** 3,667g, 1,994n, 2,765 dwt.
D 391.1 (119.21) oa, 357 (108.81) x 49.1 (14.97) x 20.1 (6.13).
E Sgl scr, oil, 7 cyls, 2 stroke sgl acting, 4,670 BHP, 16½ kts. By M.A.N., Augsberg.
H Steel. 2 dks + pt 3rd. 4 hatches. 217,195 cu ft (6,150.3 cu m)g, 191,656 cu ft (5,427 cu m) refrig.
1956 Feb 24: Launched as *Parthenon* for Laiesz & Co, Africanische Frucht-Cie. Fruit carrier inbound general cargo out between Hamburg and Tika, Cameroons.
1962 Chartered to Geest Industries for Barry—Preston—West Indies route.
1964 Sept: Acquired by Blue Star and r/n *Padova Star*. Mediterranean—South America service.
1966 Transferred to Calmedia S.p.A. di Nav, Cagliari; renamed *Calarossa*, same route.
1974 Sold to Nogrou Navigation Co, Limassol. R/n *Imperia*. The owner's name was re-styled as Gofrou Navigation shortly afterwards.
1980 Oct 22: Arrived at Gadani Beach and scrapped by Paruma International.

123 **BARCELONA STAR**
Details as *Padova Star* (112) except: **B** 1955. **T** 4,705g. **D** 393.3ft (119.88m) oa.
1954 Dec 8: Launched.
1955 Delivered as *Piraus* for Laiesz & Co's Africanische Frucht Cie.
1965 Jan: Acquired by Blue Star to become *Barcelona Star*. Mediterranean—South America service. She made the fifth vessel in the service.
1965 Transferred as *Calasetta* to Calmedia S.p.A. di Nav. Same service.

1974 Sold to Nogrou Navigation Co, Limassol. R/n *Sanstefano*.
1976 Her operators became Norfo Cia Nav S.A., Panama; same name and owning group.
1981 May: Laid up at Bombay pending sale for breaking up. Nov: Scrapped at Darukhana by Gokalchand & Co.

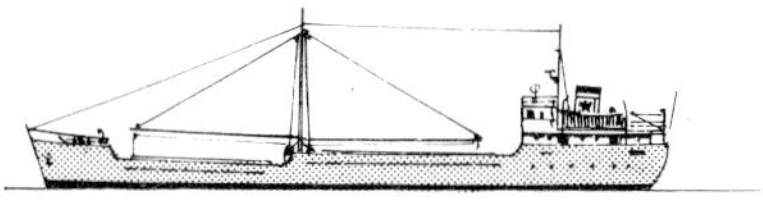

WAVENEY STAR/WAVENEY

124 **WAVENEY STAR/WAVENEY**
B 1956 Schpsw, Bodewes Gruno, Foxhol. **T** 487g, 281n, 670 dwt.
D 169 (51.51) oa, 154.1 (46.97) x 27.5 (8.38) x 11.2 (3.41).
E Sgl scr, 6 cyls, 4 stroke sgl acting, 395 BHP, 9 kts. By Motorenwerke, Mannheim.
H Steel. 1 dk. F 23 (7.01). Q 58 (17.68). P 40 (12.19).
1956 Sept: Built as *Orient*, Rederij Vebo, Groningen and managed, like so many single ship owners, by Kamps Scheep & Handel N.V.
1961 R/n *Zaandijk* by her owner while on charter to N.V. Solleveld's S. & A. Maats.
1962 Reverted to *Orient* and the same managers.
1964 Acquired by Blue Star Line Ltd to operate their U.K. and Continental ports—London feeder service. R/n *Waveney Star*.
1965 Became *Waveney*, Blue Star Line; managed by G. T. Gillie & Blair Ltd.
1970 Sold to D. P. Kalkassinas, Thessaloniki. R/n *Meropi*.
1975 Owned by Zissis Triantafyllou & G. Topalis; same name and port.
1985 Dec: R/n *Stelios A*, Nikolas Kritsinaris then *Stelios Amorgianos*.
1988 Apr: Still in service.

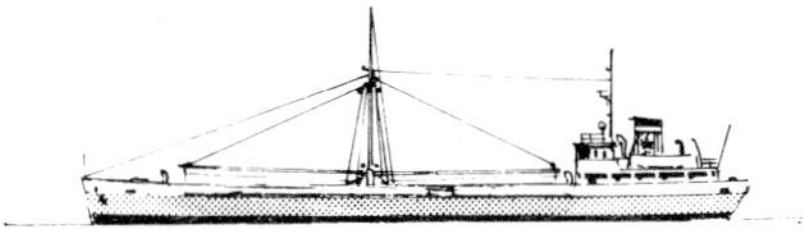

ORWELL STAR/ORWELL

125 **ORWELL STAR/ORWELL**
B 1956 Scheepsw J. G. Bijholt, Foxhol. **T** 495,314n, 660 dwt.
D 173.2 (52.79) oa, 160 (48.77) x 28.6 (8.72) x 10.4 (3.17).
E Sgl scr, oil, 6 cyls, 4 stroke sgl acting, 395 BHP, 10 kts. By Motorenwerke, Mannheim.
H Steel. 1 dk. 2 hatches.
1956 Feb: Built as *Julia-Anna* for E. Smid, N.V. Carebeka managers. Later by N.V. Gruno.
1965 Purchased and renamed *Orwell Star* for Tyne—Middlesbrough—Humber—London feeder service.
1966 Renamed *Orwell* and placed under the management of G. T. Gillie Blair Ltd. The ship still bore Blue Star livery.
1968 Sold to S. Wm. Coe & Co Ltd, Liverpool; renamed *Booker Trader* and operated by Booker Shipping (Demerara) Ltd.
1975 Her owners became Booker Line Ltd.
1977 Purchased by the Ministry of Works & Transport, Government of Guyana. R/n *Guytrader*.
1982 Became *Guy Trader*, Guyana National Shipping Corp Ltd, Georgetown.
1988 Still in service.

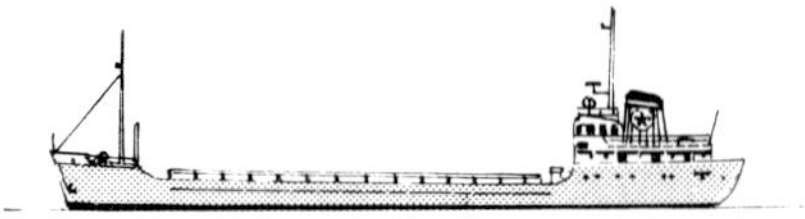

CROUCH, DEBEN

126 **CROUCH**
B 1966 Boele's Schps & Mchf, Bolnes, Netherlands. **T** 500g, 289n, 756 dwt.
D 183.5 (55.94) oa, 165.4 (50.42) x 28.8 (8.79) x 10.9 (3.34).
E Sgl scr, oil, 6 cyls, 4 stroke sgl acting, 530 BHP, 10½ kts. By Blackstone & Co, Stamford. Fitted with a variable pitch propeller.
H Steel. 1 dk. F 24.3 (7.4). P 40 (12.2). 1 hold, 37,000 cu ft (1,048 cu m)g.
1966 Apr 19: Launched for Blue Star as *Crouch*. May: Managed by G. T. Gillie & Blair Ltd. The feeder service vessels under Gillie Blair management carried no 'Star' suffix.
1971 Sold to Mardorf, Peach & Co Ltd. R/n *Camilla Weston*. G. T. Gillie & Blair remained managers.
1976 The owners became Weston Shipping but then reverted to their former name.
1984 Feb 15: Run down in fog by *Larissasee* (Larissasee Intersee, German) while at anchor off Happisburgh enroute Leith with grain. Sank.

127 DEBEN
Sister to *Crouch* (126) except: **T** 500g.
1966 Feb 18: Launched as *Deben*. Managed by G. T. Gillie Blair Ltd. March: Delivered.
1971 Sold to Mardorf, Peach & Co Ltd; renamed *Gretchen Weston* with the same managers.
1976 Became *Ben Ain,* Ramsey S.S. Co, Isle of Man.
1988 Still in service.

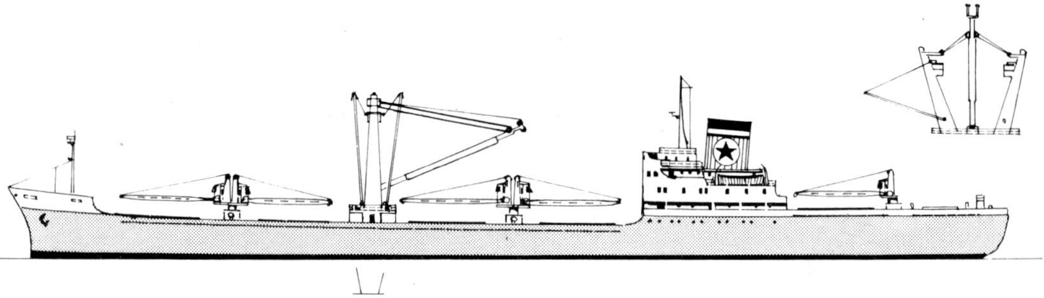

AUSTRALIA STAR (II)

128 **AUSTRALIA STAR (II)**
B 1965 Austin & Pickersgill Ltd, Sunderland. **T** 10,025g, 5,842n, 12,170 dwt.
D 526.1 (160.36) obb, 485 (147,83) x 70.1 (21.37(x 30 (9.14).
E Sgl scr, oil, 8 cyls, Sulzer, 17,600 BHP, 19 kts. By Vickers Armstrong (Eng) Ltd, Barrow-in-Furness, transported to Sunderland for installation.
H Steel. 2 dks + pt 3rd. F 42 (12.8). P 190 (57.91). 5 hatches.
C 626,020 cu ft (17,727 cu m)g, 109,200 cu ft (3092.2 cu m)ins. Derricks 1 x 300 ton Stulcken.
1965 May 11: Launched. Dec: After completion the ship was towed to Hamburg for the fitting of her 300 ton Stülcken jumbo derrick which was, at the time, the largest lift ever to be fitted to a merchant vessel. (See *South Africa Star* (77)). May: Entered service.
1972 Chartered to Chr. Haaland, Norway. R/n *Concordia Star*.
1974 Off charter. R/n *Australia Star*. Apr: Sold to Costa Armatori S.p.A. Naples. R/n *Cortina*.
1984 Became *Candy Ace*, Jetset Shipping Corp, Panama.
1985 Apr 4: Arrived at Shanghai for scrapping.

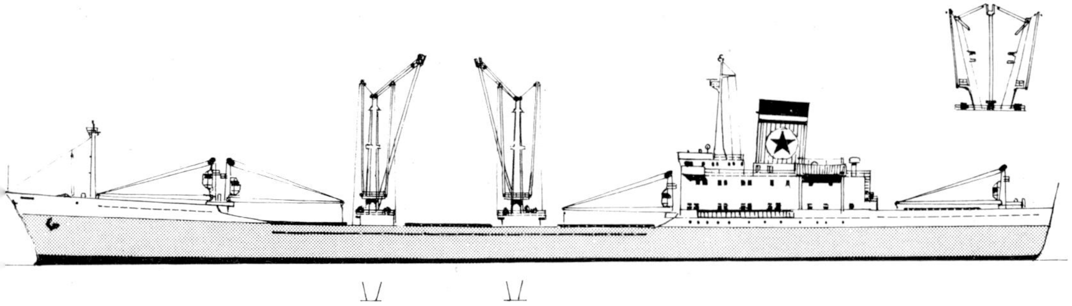

A. SOUTHLAND STAR, NEW ZEALAND STAR (II)/WELLINGTON STAR

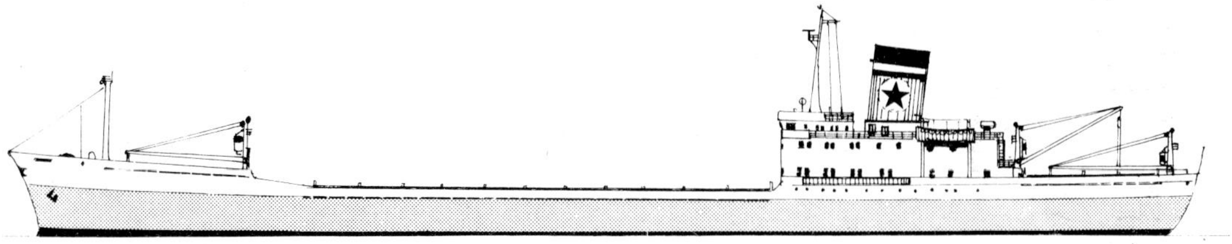

B. SOUTHLAND STAR, NEW ZEALAND STAR (II)/WELLINGTON STAR (III)

129 **SOUTHLAND STAR**
B 1967 Bremer Vulkan S.u M, Bremen-Vegesack. **T** 11,300g, 6,627n, 13,470 dwt.
D 552.3 (168.34) obb, 515.9 (157.25) x 73.3 (22.34) x 29.3 (8.93).
E Sgl scr, oil, 9 cyls, 2 stroke sgl acting, M.A.N. type K9Z86/160E, 21 kts. By builder.
H Steel. 2 dks + pt 3 & 4. F 113 (34.44). P 198 (66.35). C 562,627 cu ft (15,931.9 cu m) refrig plus containers. 130,000 cu ft (3,681 cu m) general.
1967 Jan 10: Launched. The engine room controls were operated from the bridge. June: Delivered for U.K.—Australia and New Zealand service. (129A).
1975 Her managers became Blue Star Ship Management Ltd.
1979 Converted to container ship (Drawing 129B).
1985 July 25: Towed the disabled yacht *Windwalker* into the safety of Hawaiian waters where U.S. Coastguards took over.
1988 March: Present fleet.

130 **NEW ZEALAND STAR (II)/WELLINGTON STAR (III)**
Details as *Southland Star* (129).
1967 May 11: Launched. Sept: Maiden voyage to New Zealand.
1970 Mar 9: During darkness a shudder ran through the ship and her speed unaccountably dropped. At daylight the dead corpse of a 40ft whale was found impaled on the bow.
1975 Managed by BSSM.
1979 Renamed *Wellington Star* in order to release the name for a new container ship. Converted to container ship.
1988 April: Present fleet.

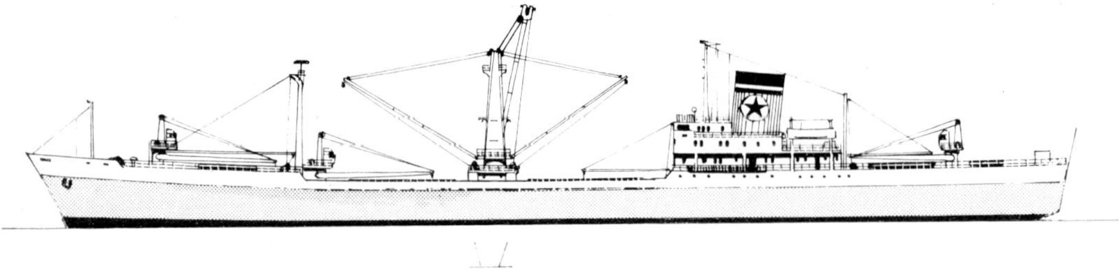

TIMARU STAR (II)

131 **TIMARU STAR (II)**
B 1967 Bartram & Sons Ltd, Sunderland. **T** 8,366g, 4,775n, 10,830 dwt.
D 496.9ft (151.45m) oa, 456.2ft (139.05m) x 65.2ft (19.87m) x 29.8ft (9.08m).
E Sgl scr, oil, 8 cyls, 2 stroke sgl acting Sulzer design, 12,000 BHP, 18 kts. By G. Clark & Co, Sunderland.
H Steel. 2 dks + pt 3rd. F 126ft (38.4m). P 190ft (57.91m). C 331,680 cu ft (9392.2 cu m)ins.
1967 Feb 26: Launched. July: Maiden voyage on the New Zealand route.
1975 Managed by BSSM.
1978 Oct 17: Her accommodation was damaged by fire at Cardiff. Two officers killed.
1984 Transferred to the subsidiary Crest Shipping Ltd, Hong Kong. R/n *Crest Hill*. New funnel design.
1985 March: Broken up at Huangpu, China.

(Drawing Page 89)

132 **CALIFORNIA STAR (III)**
B 1971 Bremer Vulkan S.u M, Bremen-Vegesack. **T** 19,095g, 10,730n, 19,114 dwt.
D 619.6ft (188.85m) obb, 584.85ft (178m) x 85ft (25.91m) x 33ft (10.06m).
E Sgl scr, oil, 9 cyls, M.A.N. type K9SZ 90/160 low speed direct coupling, 26,100 BHP, 21½ kts. By builder. **H** Steel. 1 dk. F 135ft (41.2m). P 159ft (48.5m).
C 218,561 cu ft (6,189 cu m)ins. 7 holds. 869 standard 20ft (6.1m) and 40ft (12.2m) containers or bin containers. The holds immediately before and that aft of the bridge superstructure are refrigerated down to -10°F; in all 125 containers. 10 holds.
1971 Jan 12: Launched. Built to operate on the Scanstar joint service with ships of the Danish concern East Asiatic Co from Europe to the West coast of North America. Her Danish consorts were the larger *Flandria* and *Meonia*.
1975 Operated by BSSM.
1987 Transferred to the Austasia Line. R/n *Mulbera*; the name coming from British India S.N. Co nomenclature.
1988 Present fleet.

133 **COLUMBIA STAR (II)**
Details as *California Star* (132).
1971 June 25: Launched; same service as her sistership.
1975 As with the rest of the fleet managed by BSSM.
1986 Nov: Transferred to the Austasia service. R/n *Mandama*; their livery.
1988 Present fleet.

(Drawing Page 89)

134 **AFRIC STAR (II)**
B 1975 Smith's Dock Co Ltd, South Bank Middlesbrough. **T** 9,784g, 5,428n, 11,092 dwt.
D 511.2 (155.8) obb, 471.4 (143.69) x 70.1 (21.37) x 28.1 (8.56).
E Sgl scr, oil, 9 cyls, 2 stroke sgl acting Kincaid—B&W type 9K74EF turbo-charged, 15,900 BHP at 120 rpm. 23 kts. By J. G. Kincaid & Co. Fuel 2,634.5 tons.
H Steel. 3 dks + pt 4th. F 50.2 (15.3). Transom stern. 5 holds. C 475,000 cu ft (13,450.6 cu m)

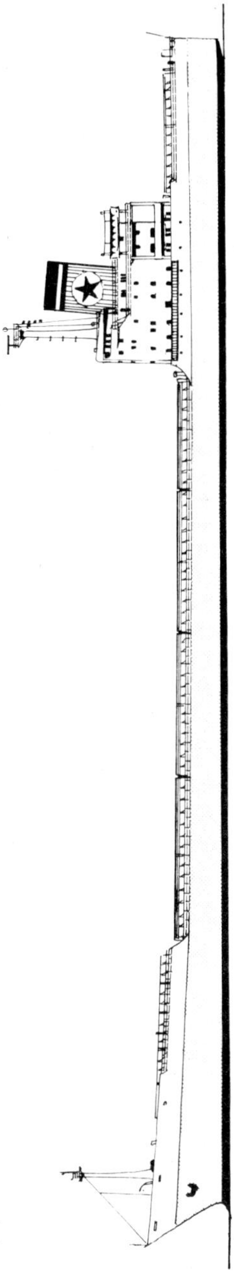

CALIFORNIA STAR (III), COLUMBIA STAR (II)

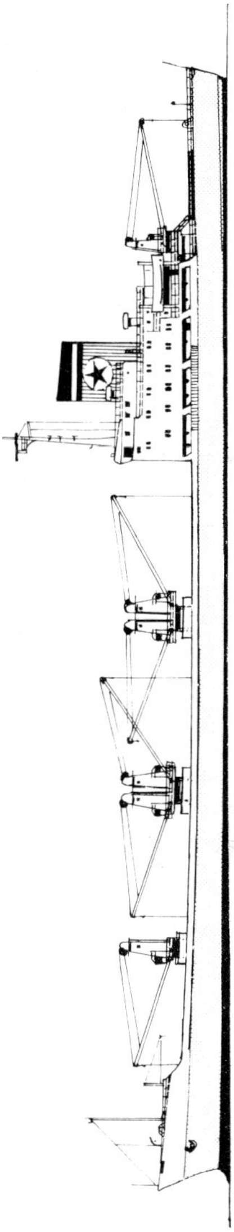

AFRIC STAR (II), AVILA STAR (II), ANDALUCIA STAR (II)
ALMERIA STAR, ALMEDA STAR (II), AVELONA STAR (II)

refrig. in 18 compartments. 6 Nylands deck cranes, Crew 36. Fruit hoists and fork lift trucks used. Carries bananas, deciduous and citrus fruits, cartoned meat, fish and dairy produce.
1973 Ordered at a fixed price of £5 million for world wide seasonal fruit tramping.
1974 Sept 3: Launched. The first of a class of six ships which carried the 'A' names of the four 1927 passenger ships. The exceptions were *Almeria Star* and *Afric Star* which replaced *Arandora Star* whose name has never been repeated. This is outside of the normal practice whereby wartime losses are usually remembered through a subsequent ship. Only marine loss is deemed by some to be unlucky.
1975 Feb: Completed. Owned by Glencairn Shipping Co Ltd. on bare-boat charter to Blue Star Line with Blue Star Ship management as managers.
1987 Sold to High Herald Ltd, Hong Kong. R/n *Lanark*; same managers.
1988 Still in service.

135 **AVILA STAR (II)**
Sister to *Afric Star* (134) except: **B** Akers Bergebs Mekaniske Verksteder with the hull being sub-contracted to A/S Nakskov Skibs, Nakstov.
T 9,766g, 5,421n, 11,093 dwt. **E** By Nylands M/V, Oslo.
1974 Nov 20: Launched.
1975 June: Delivered to Blue Star Line Ltd. Blue Star Ship Management Ltd.
1979 Became *Hidlefjord*, Kornelius Olsen, Stavanger.
1988 Still in service.

136 **ANDALUCIA STAR (II)**
Sister to *Afric Star* (134) except: **T** 9,784g.
1975 June 14: Named. The day was so windy that the actual launch had to be postponed until the following day. Blue Star Ship Management Ltd. Berthed at the Pool of London, the largest vessel to do so, but only as a public relations exercise.
1977 June 5: Rescued the crew of the burning *Ain Leuh* of South Korea and landed them at Las Palmas. Later chartered to Union Castle Line for their South African service and painted in their colours.
1982 Chartered by the British Government for use as a Falklands floating general supply ship 'The Floating Supermarket'. A helicopter pad was fitted aft at Tilbury. Funnel colouring: white, black and white bands, black top; viz the red portion and blue star painted white.
1985 Sold to Highvale Ltd, Wallem Shipmanagement Ltd, Hong Kong; renamed *Fife*. Still in service on long term, bare-boat charter to Blue Star.

137 **ALMERIA STAR**
Sister to *Afric Star* (134) except: **B** 1976. **T** 9,781g, 5,416n, 11,093 dwt.
1976 July 13: Launched for Transport Exchange Co Ltd on bare-boat charter to Blue Star. Her name was a new 'A' for the fleet. Nov: Entered service; BSSM as managers.
1984 June 14: Collided with Cunard's *Servia* off Zeebrugge enroute Antwerp—Sheerness; repaired at Flushing.
1984 Acquired by the New Prestige Ltd, Wallem Shipmanagement Ltd, Hong Kong. R/n *Perth*. On charter to Blue Star Line.
1985 July: Laid up in the River Blackwater. Her owners became High Herald Ltd; same managers.
1986 Out of lay up and overhauled at Falmouth.
1988 Still in service.

138 **ALMEDA STAR (II)**
Sister to *Afric Star* (134) except: **B** 1976. **T** 9,781g, 5,416n, 11,092 dwt.
1976 Apr: Delivered to Avelona Star Ltd on bare-boat charter to Blue Star Ltd. Operated by BSSM.
1984 June: Sold to Arran Shipping Ltd. Wallem Shipmanagement Ltd managers, Hong Kong.

R/n *Arran*. Chartered to Blue Star. July: Final Blue Star sailing then laid up in the River Blackwater.
1985 R/n *Harlech*; same managers. Back in service; fruit tramping.
1988 In service.

139 **AVELONA STAR (II)**
Sister to *Afric Star* (134) except: **B** 1975. **T** 9,784g, 5,428n, 11,092 dwt.
1975 Dec: Delivered to Avelona Star Ltd. Managers Blue Star Ship Management Ltd.
1982 Chartered with her sister *Andalucia Star* for Falklands duty.
1985 Became *Castle Peak*, Stirling Ltd, Wallem Shipmanagement, Hong Kong. On charter to Blue Star Line.
1988 Still in service.

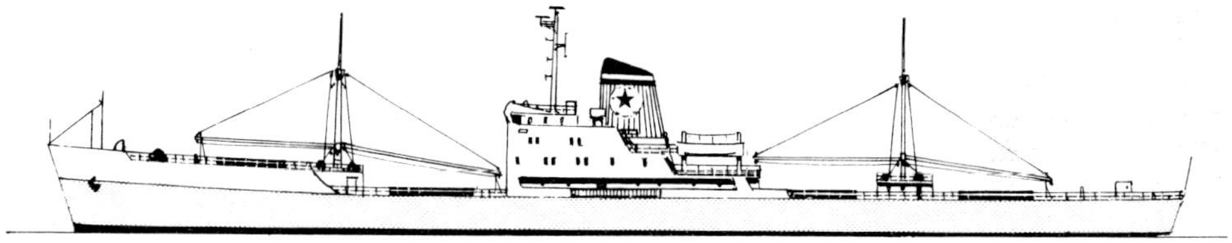

TUSCAN STAR (III), TROJAN STAR (II)

140 **TUSCAN STAR (III)**
B 1972 Drammen Slip & Verk, Drammen. **T** 6,671g, 3,641n, 9,094 dwt.
D 461.4 (140.62) oa, 432.7 (131.88) x 59.2 (18.04) x 29.7 (9.04).
E Sgl scr, oil, 9 cyls, Sulzer type, 14,850 BHP, 23 kts. By builder.
H Steel. 4 dks. F 82 (25). 2 hatches. C 353,533 cu ft (10,011 cu m)ins.
1972 Jan 23: Launched. May: Delivered as *Labrador Clipper* for Maritime Fruit Carriers and operated by Chichester Shipping Lines Ltd, Glasgow.
1976 The group ran into financial difficulties and the ships had to be disposed of. July 27: Purchased from Maritime Midland Bank Ltd, the mortgagees, and renamed *Tuscan Star*. Operated by Blue Star Ship Management Ltd; registered at Glasgow.
1980 Became *Chios Pride*, Sun Glory Compania Naviera S.A., Piraeus. (Diana Shipping Agencies).
1988 Still in service.

141 **TROJAN STAR (II)**
Details as *Tuscan Star* (140) except: **B** 1972 Smith's Dockyard Co, South Bank-on-Tees. **E** By Clark & N.E.M. Ltd, Sunderland. **H** C 352,297 cu ft (9,976 cu m)ins.
1972 Nov 20: Launched as *Newcastle Clipper* for Maritime Fruit Carriers' subsidiary Rockhampton Shipping Co.
1973 March: Entered service in the name of Sovetur Shipping Co with North West Shipping Co, Glasgow, as managers.
1976 July 27: Acquired with her sister ship. R/n *Trojan Star*. Managed by BSSM.
1980 June 12: Disabled 800 miles off New Zealand with rudder failure during a gale. Towed by the tug *Raumanga* 747 miles to Wellington. June 24: Arrived. Oct. Trapped for some weeks at Bandar Khomeini during the Iran-Iraq war.
1981 Sold to Saful Navigation Co, Greece with Diana Shipping Agencies as managers. R/n *Chios Clipper*.
1988 Still in service.

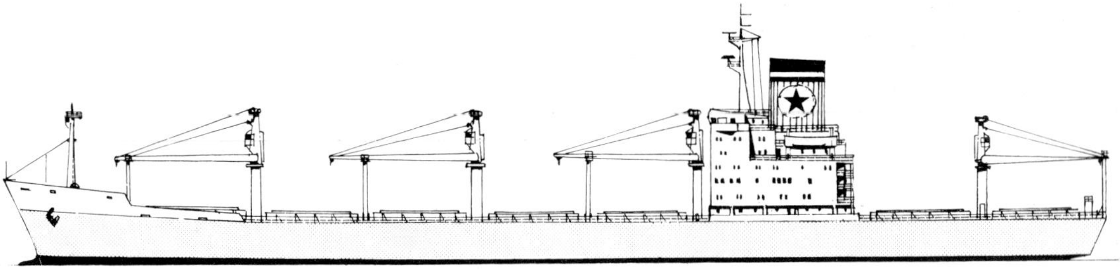

AUSTRALIA STAR (III), NEW ZEALAND STAR (III)

142 **AUSTRALIA STAR (III)**
B 1978 Smith's Dock Co Ltd. **T** 17,082g, 8,930n, 16,114 dwt.
D 554 (168.87) obb, 527 (160.61) x 82.68 (25.2) x 30.7 (9.37).
E Sgl scr, oil, 6 cyls Sulzer, 17,400 BHP, 18 kts. (at 15,500 BHP).
By Barclay Curle, Whiteinch, Glasgow.
H Steel. 1 dk. F 66.27 (20.2m) C 293,570 cu ft (8,313 cu m)ins. 721 containers: 308 reefer and 413 general.
1978 Apr 22: Launched. Aug: Delivered to Brodies (London) Ltd. Blue Star Ship Management Ltd as managers. The cost of these two container ships was £30 million including the additional port back up facilities involved.
1988 Present fleet.

143 **NEW ZEALAND STAR (III)**
Sister to *Australia Star* (142) except: **B** 1979.
1978 July 20: Launched for Blue Star Line Ltd. BSSM as managers. Container capacity 721 TEU's.
1979 Jan: Entered service.
1986 Jan 5: Arrived at Singapore from New Plymouth. Lengthened by the insertion of a new centre section, by Jurong shipyard. Capacity raised to 1,151 TEU's. Repainted in Lamport & Holt colours for their South American Brisa service. April: Positioned in ballast to Montevideo for the loaded homeward voyage. May 12: Renamed *Churchill* at Tilbury by Lady Soames, Sir Winston Churchill's daughter. She was replaced on Blue Star's Antipodes—Persian Gulf service by *Columbia Star* (133). The statistics of her service to New Plymouth has been recorded: Calls 1979-1985: 42. Containers: Discharged 4,766 laden, 8,047 empty. Loaded: 7,824 laden. 136 empty. Restowed during the process: 2,548. Total 23,321 moved. The working time was 1,180.6 hours at 19.75 TEU's per hour. The total lapsed hours (night and day) in port were 2331,2 to give an operating average of 10 TEU's per hour—one every six minutes. This clearly demonstrates the effectiveness of containerisation. No other form of handling dry goods can match this rate of cargo movement.
1988 Still in service.

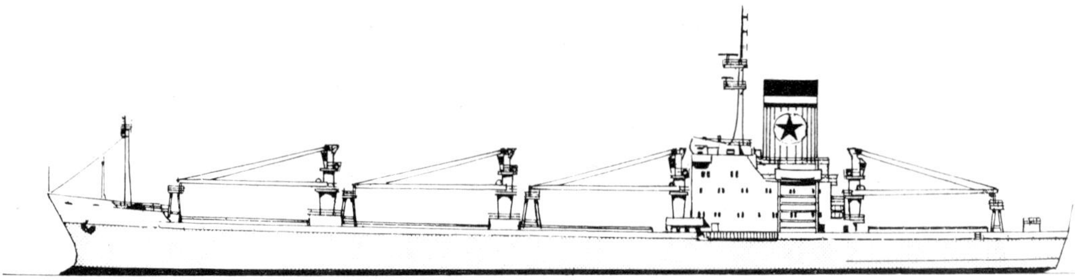

SCOTTISH STAR (III), ENGLISH STAR (II), AUCKLAND STAR (III), CANTERBURY STAR (II)

144 **SCOTTISH STAR (II)**
B 1985 Harland & Wolff, Belfast. **T** 10,291g, 5,398n, 13,058 dwt.
D 495.4 (151.01) oa x 72.18 (22) x 41.7 (12.7). Dft 30.5 (9.3).
E Sgl scr, oil, 2S.SA, B&W type, 22,000 BHP. 20 kts service speed. By builder. Engine controlled from the bridge. **H** Steel. 2 + part 3rd dk. C 463,000 cu ft (13,111 cu m) refrig for meat, citrus fruits, bananas or refrigerated TEU's. Crew 21. Swimming pool abaft funnel.
1983 Ordered. All four ships were built simultaneously in the same dry dock at a cost of £80 million. They were to be floated at the same time and finished at adjacent berths. With their delivery the five year charter of the Tokumaru four (153-156) would be released.
1985 March 28: Named, none were 'launched'. Apr 2: Completed for Lombard Leasing Metropolitan Ltd on long term bare-boat charter to Blue Star Line Ltd with BSSM as managers. She was a month ahead of schedule in order to compensate for the late delivery of her fire-damaged sister. This enabled her to make two fruit delivery voyages before the season's end in May 1985.
1988 Present fleet.

145 **ENGLISH STAR (II)**
As 144.
1984 Dec 16: A fire in the engine room caused damage of over £1 million and delayed completion by six months. This led to *Scottish Star* entering service first. Same owners and status.
1985 Jan 25: Named on schedule. Feb: Original delivery date. Nov 19: Completed.
1986 Jan 6: Trials. Jan 15: Left Belfast for St. Nazaire and maiden voyage.
1987 Renamed *Hornsea*. On charter to Horn Linie, Hamburg, until January 1989. Their livery.
1988 Still in service.

146 **AUCKLAND STAR (III)**
As 144.
1985 Nov 5: Named. Owners: Investors in Industry PLC. On long term bare-boat charter with BSSM as managers.
1987 Renamed *Horncliff*. On charter to Horn Linie, Hamburg until January 1989. Their livery.
1988 Still in service.

147 **CANTERBURY STAR (II)**
As 144.
1985 Dec 11: Named. Owned by Investors in Industry PLC.
1988 Present fleet.

CHARTERED VESSELS OPERATED IN BLUE STAR LIVERY WITH BLUE STAR NAMES

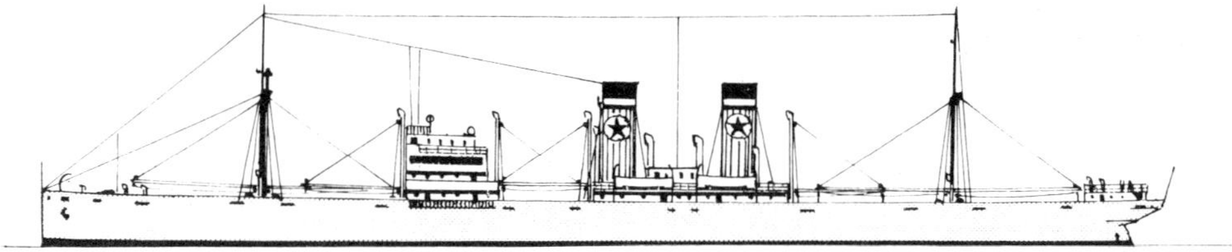

YAKIMA STAR, WENATCHEE STAR

148 **YAKIMA STAR**
B 1929 Deutsches Werke, Kiel. **T** 6,660g, 4,164n.
D 461.3ft (140.6m) x 60.6ft (18.47m) x 27.3ft (8.32m).
E Tw scr, oil, 12 cyls, 2 stroke dbl acting, 16 kts. By builder. **H** Steel. 1 dk and shelter dk + pt 3rd.
1928 Feb 18: Launched. June 18: Trials. June 24: Delivered. Built as *Sud Americano*, Linea Sud Americano, Invar An Christensen, Oslo.

1930 Returned to the builders on the grounds that the ship did not meet her loaded speed specifications,. On trials this had been met. Speculation was that the world depression contributed to the decision. Renamed *Schleswig* and laid up at Kiel.
1931 Chartered to Blue Star Line as *Yakima Star*; returned to builders at the end of the year. Laid up at Kiel.
1934 Sold to Hanseatische Schiffs und Betriebs (Norddeutscher Lloyd) and renamed *Weser*. Rebuilt with single funnel and new M.A.N. diesels.
1937 Transferred to Norddeutscher Lloyd; same name.
1940 Sept 25: Captured by H.M.C.S. *Prince Robert* off Pacific coast of Mexico. Renamed *Vancouver Island*, Canadian Government Merchant Marine.
1941 Oct 15: 23.17 hrs. Torpedoed by *U-558* en route Quebec—Belfast.

149 **WENATCHEE STAR**
Details and history as *Yakima Star* (148) except: **B** 1929. **T** 6,607g, 4,158n.
1929 Built as *Sud Expresso*.
1930 Renamed *Holstein*, laid up at Kiel.
1931 On charter to Blue Star as *Wenatchee Star* for nine months.
1934 Renamed *Elbe* for Hanseatische S.u.B; rebuilt.
1937 Transferred to Norddeutscher Lloyd; same name.
1941 June 6: Sunk off the Azores by aircraft from the aircraft carrier *Eagle*.

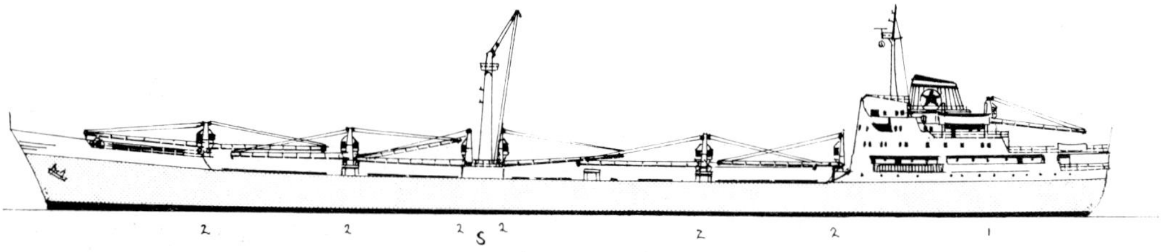

OAKLAND STAR (II)

150 **OAKLAND STAR (II)**
B 1966 Kherson Shipyard, Kherson, USSR. **T** 9,854g, 5,513n, 13,254 dwt.
D 510.9ft (155.72m) oa, 459.3ft (140m) x 67.8ft (20.67m) x 40.3ft (12.3m).
ESgl scr, oil, 7 cyls, 2 stroke sgl acting, 8,750 BHP, 18 kts. By Bryansk Eng Works, Bryansk.
H Steel. 2 dks. F 92ft (28.04m) P 108ft (32.92m) C.
1966 Completed as *Klavdia*, Klavdia Cia Nav, Piraeus.
1969 Chartered by Blue Star; renamed *Oakland Star*.
1971 Reverted to *Klavdia* at the termination of the charter.
1973 Aug 2: Aground at Chittagong inbound from Chicago. Aug 10: Refloated.
1981 Sold to New Delta Maritime Co S.A., Panama; renamed *Union Hamburg* then *Hotagen*.
1983 Became *Balstad*, Pasture Navigation Corp, Panama.
1984 Oct 21: Broken up by Keun Hwa Iron Works & Enterprise Co, Kaohsiung.

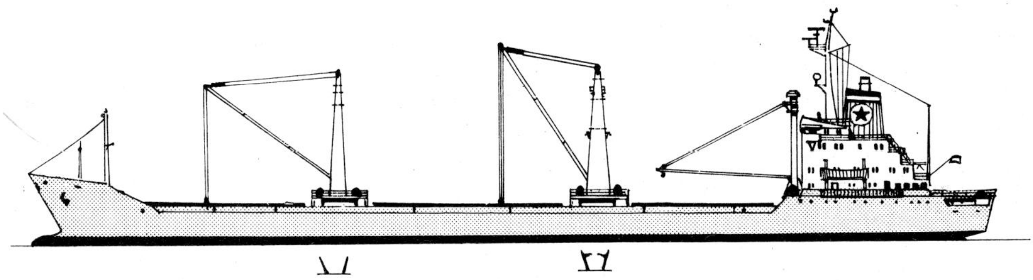

ALBION STAR (III)

151 **ALBION STAR (III)**
B 1972 Orenstein, Koppel and Lübecker Masch, Lübeck. **T** 8,329g, 5,696n, 12,000 dwt.
D 471.8ft (143.8m) obb x 70.7ft (21.54m) x 23.2ft (7.07m).
E Sgl scr, Vee oil, 18 cyls, 4 stroke Pielstick sgl acting with reduction gearing, 9,630 BHP, 18 kts. By Blohm & Voss, Hamburg. **H** Steel. 2 dks. F 36ft (11m). B 69.2ft (21.1m).
C 386 TEU's of which 132 ref. Derricks 2 x 35 ton, 1 x 22 ton, 6 x 10 ton.
1972 Built as *Rheingold* for Cosima Reederei K.G., with Poseidon Schiffahrt G.m.b.H. as operators.
1973 Renamed *Columbus California*; same owners.
1979 Reverted to *Rheingold*, Ernst Willner G.m.b.H., managers.
1982 Jan 10: Chartered to Blue Star; renamed *Albion Star*. Replaced *Rockhampton Star* and *Gladstone Star* on the 'British Line Service' to South America. Her consort is *Devon* chartered by Royal Mail.
1985 Reverted to *Rheingold*, Cosima Reederei K.G. Managed by Coronado Schiffahrts.

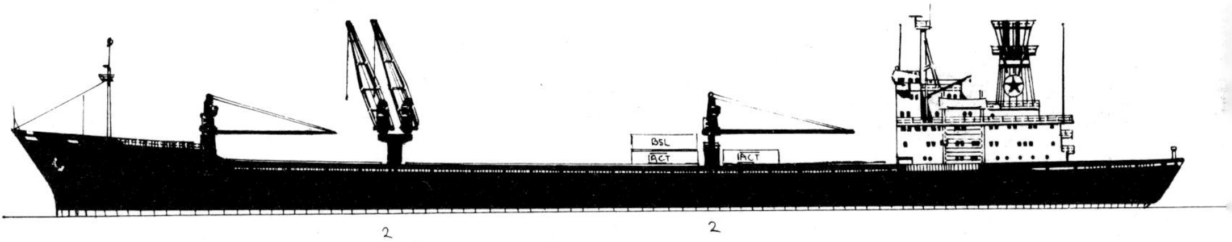

SAXON STAR (III)

152 **SAXON STAR (III)**
B 1976 Kherson Works, Kherson. **T** 11,800g, 7,064n, 15,500 dwt.
D 531.5ft (162.31m) oa, x 72.9ft (22.2m) x 33.2ft (10.12m).
E Sgl scr, oil, 6 cyls, sgl acting, 11,600 BHP, Burmeister & Wain type. 18¾ kts.
By Bryansk Engine Works, Bryansk.
H Steel. 2 dks. Container ship; 276 below deck, 120 on deck and 35 aft, of these 315 are refrigerated.
1976 Built as *Santa Rita* for Hamburg Sud-Americanische D.G., Eggert & Amsinck; South American service. One of the Russain *Dnepr* class.
1979 Became *Columbus Taranaki*, same owners. Converted to a container ship from general cargo. Pacific Coast of North America service.
1980 Name changed to *Monte Olivia*; same owners South American service.
1982 Renamed *Columbus California*; same owners. North Pacific service.
1983 Wet-charter to Blue Star Line Ltd; renamed *Saxon Star*; same owners. Operates on the BHLR service. BHLR = Blue Star, Houlder, Lamport & Holt and Royal Mail.
1986 Reverted to *Columbus California*; original ownership.

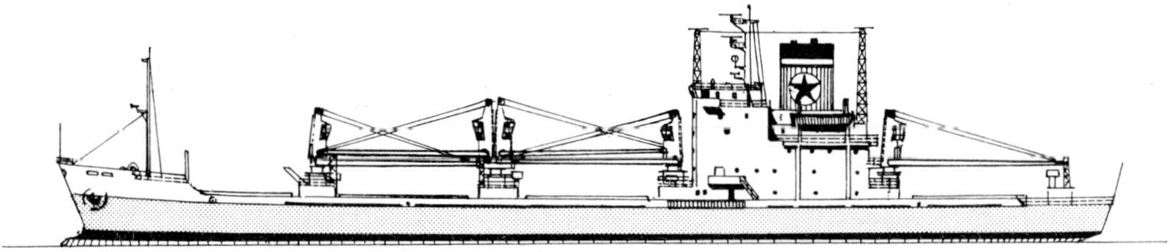

BALTIC STAR, TASMAN STAR, ATLANTIC STAR, PACIFIC STAR (IV)

153 **BALTIC STAR**
B 1983 Sasebo Heavy Industries, Saebo. **T** 9,628g, 4,045n, 9,464 dwt.
D 460.9ft (140.49m) obb x 72.8ft (22.2m) x 33ft (10m).
E Sgl scr, oil, direct drive. 20,000 BHP, 22½ kts. By builder.
H Steel. 2 dks. C 39,767 cu ft (111,261 cu m) refrig. 54 TEU's.
1983 Jan 9: Launched for Tokumaru Kaium Kaisha but wet-boat chartered to Blue Star for five years and entered service as *Baltic Star*. Operated and crewed by Tokumaru K.K. Corn yellow hull.
1988 In service.

154 **TASMAN STAR**
Details and chartering arrangements as *Baltic Star*.
1983 Jan 27: Launched. Owned by Makoto Senpaku K.K; Tokumaru as managers. Details of charter as *Baltic Star*.
1988 Still in service.

155 **ATLANTIC STAR**
1983 Jan 28: Launched. On charter to Blue Star Line with Tokumaru as managers.
1988 Still in service.

156 **PACIFIC STAR (IV)**
1983 Jan 31: Launched for Tokumaru U.K. on charter to Blue Star Line.
1988 Still in service but all four finish their five year charter early in the year.

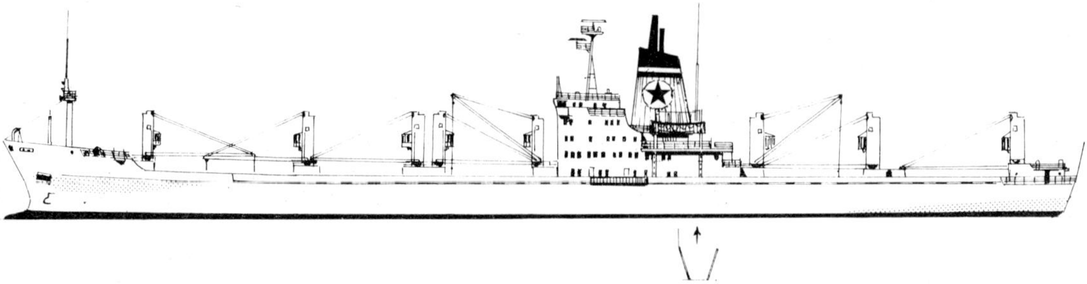

SANTOS STAR (II), SAVONA STAR

157 **SANTOS STAR (II)**
B 1972 Chantiers Navals de la Ciotat, La Ciotat. **T** 11,422g, 5,052n, 12,782 dwt.
D 568.5 (173.3) obb x 81 (24.89) x 31.4 (10.3).
E Sgl scr, oil, 2S.SA 8 cyls Sulzer, 8RND90 type, 23,200 BHP (at 122 rpm), 22.75 kts.
By Cie de Const Mecaniquue Procédés Sulzer, Nantes.

H Steel. 4 + part 5th dk. F 62 (18.9). Side loading doors. 5 holds/hatches. 8 x 5 ton ASEA cranes. C 611,611.4 cu ft (17,319 cu m) refrig. in 22 chambers (down to -25°C). 800 BHP bow thruster.
1972 March: Built as *Snow Flake*, Saleninvest A/B; managers Salen Reefer Services A/B Stockholm. One of eight by the same yard for world wide trading. Radius 15,000 miles. Found to be a little too large in service; many loads from fruit zones were smaller than the ship's capacity necessitating additional calls with consequent cost.
1984 With the financial problems facing Salen Rederi sold to South View Shipping, Hong Kong. R/n *South View*. Panama flag.
1985 Became *Blue Sea*, Cool Ship Management, Hong Kong.
1986 Taken on charter by Blue Star Line. R/n *Santos Star*, Minolta Corporation, Hong Kong. Blue Star funnel. White livery, yellow deck cranes. Transferred to Lion Shipping Ltd, Hong Kong management. R/n *Limari*. Same owners, service and colours.
1988 Still in service.

158 **SAVONA STAR**
Details as *Santos Star* except: **B** 1973.
1973 Aug: Delivered to Salen Reefer Services A/B, Stockholm, as *Snow Ball*.
1981 Owned by Trans Malayan Shipping Inc, Manila. R/n *Malayan Queen*. Managed by Salen.
1985 Became *South Joy*, South Joy Shipping Inc, Panama.
1986 Renamed *Savona Star*, Miralta Corporation, Panama. Chartered to Blue Star. Same livery as her sister.
1988 Still in service.

MINISTRY OF DEFENCE

Blue Star Ship Management Ltd acted as managers for two Ministry of Defence vessels during and after the Falkland Islands war.
1982 April 2: 10,000 Argentine troops invaded and took the Falkland Islands.
May 20: British toops landed at San Carlos Water. June 14: The conflict ended with the surrender of General Menendez and his forces. The two ships involved, which never bore Blue Star livery were:

RANGATIRA
1982 May 15: Chartered by the M.O.D., from Union S.S. Co of New Zealand. Used as an accommodation ship off Port Stanley.
1983 October: Back in the U.K. Refitted for civilian work.
1984 March 31: BSSM management ended after the arrival of the ship for lay up in the River Fal.

KEREN
Formerly the British Railway's Sealink steamer *St Edmund*.
1983 Feb: Chartered and then purchased by M.O.D. and converted by Tyne Shiprepair Ltd into a troopship, with helicopter pad aft, to serve the Falklands until the airport became operational for troop transport aircraft. BSSM were appointed managers, known as a STUFT ship (ship taken up from trade; of which there were 66).
April 1: Due to a strike the ship was commissioned as H.M.S. *Keren* with a naval crew.
April 8: Government determination having settled the strike the vessel reverted to the Red Ensign and BSSM management, *Keren* was first used to repatriate the last of the Argentinian troops (used to clear minefields etc). She then acted as mother ship to H.M. Submarine *Opportune* before commencing her trooping voyages between Ascension Island and King Edward Cove, Port Stanley.
1984 May: Returned to the Tyne for a 12 day refit at Smiths Shiprepairers North Shields Ltd.
1985 June 20: Arrived back at Portsmouth for decommissioning. In all twenty-seven round voyages were made covering 90,000 miles and carrying 18,000 passengers, mainly military.

COMPAGNIE GÉNÉRALE FRIGORIFIQUE (C.G.F.)

1915 To cater for the export of frozen meat from Madagascar the Compagnie Générale Frigorifique was established at Majunga, where a cold store was set up to act as a collecting centre prior to loading into Blue Star vessels. In Madagascar cattle raising was spread along the coastal plains and for the task of shipping the animals to Majunga two small coasters and two lighters were ordered in 1914.
1920 With the ending of the war in Europe French interests again predominated in this French possession and Blue Star had, themselves, reverted to their traditional routes to New Zealand, Australia and the Argentine. French shipping companies—such as Messageries Maritimes—took over the export trade in Madagascar and Cie Gen Frigorifique was closed down and its four vessels sold locally to perform the same duties.

FLEET

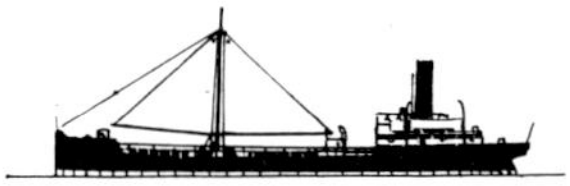

GENERAL PAU, GENERAL FOCH

159 **GENERAL PAU**
B 1915 Montrose Shipbuilding Co, Montrose. **T** 254g, 120n.
D 126ft (28.4m) bp x 25.2ft (7.68m) x 5ft (2.43m).
E Sgl scr, tpl exp, 3 cyls, 9 kts. By Wm Beardmore & Co, Glasgow.
H Steel. 1 dk. C Live cattle, tinned meat and fruit.
1914 Ordered by Blue Star Line Ltd prior to the formation of C.G.F. Technically it can be claimed that this ship was the first newbuilding for the company because *Brodhurst* (9) was purchased on the stocks.
1915 June: Transferred to C.G.F. before completion. Fitted for towage.
1920 Transferred, with the business, to Compagnie de Transportes et Remorquages de Madagascar (Transport & Towage Co of Madagascar). Same name.
1958 Sold to Societe Industrielle de la Côte Ouest de Madagascar.
1969 Owned, same name, by Mons M. Verdier and operated Majunja—Comoro Is. Reputedly still in service. No trace in Lloyd's nor any change in name.

160 **GENERAL FOCH**
Sister to *General Pau* (159) except: **B** 1916. **T** 248g.
1916 June: Built for C.G.F. Equipped for towing.
1920 Owned by Transportes et Remorquages de Majunga.
1957 Owned by J. Verdavainne et Cie, Majunga. Renamed *Djema*. Coastal trade.
1959 Dec 8: Wrecked off Maroni, Madagascar.

161 **GENERAL JARVONI**
B 1916 Methil. **T** 233g. **E** Lighter. **H** Steel. 1 dk.
1916 Sept 16: Left Methil in tow for Majunga. Nov 8: Arrived. Built with a double deck of caging for the carriage of live cattle to the abattoirs at Majunga. Towed by local tug or either of the powered sisters. Crew accommodation was aft,
1920 Sold with the remainder of the business to Cie de Transportes et Remorquage de Majunga. No further trace but operated for at least 20 years.

162 **GENERAL MARCUS**
Details and career as *General Jarvoni.*

SOCIEDAD ANONIMA FRIGORIFICO 'ANGLO'
Buenos Aires

The two ships owned by this subsidiary of Blue Star bore their colours and were used for the collection of frozen meat from River Plate ports.

163 **ANGLO No. 1**
B 1921 Cammell Laird & Co, Birkenhead. **T** 1,354g, 795n.
D 220.5ft (67.21m) bp x 44.1ft (13.44m) x 9.3ft (30.5m).
E Tw scr, 2 x 2 cyl comp inverted, 50 NHP, 9 kts. By builder.
H Steel. Flush 1 dk with engines aft. Refrig.
1921 Built as *Zarate* for Union Cold Storage, Frigorifico as managers.
1922 Renamed *Shirley* and in the same year *Kingswood*, Sir William Vestey having become Baron Kingswood.
1923 Renamed *Anglo No. 1*.
1938 Frigorifico became the owners.
1960 Sold to Naviero Panamericano S.A. as *Santa Teresa*.
1966 Passed to Intervariou S.A. Cia, Buenos Aires. Same name. Broken up at Buenos Aires.

164 **ANGLO No. 2**
B 1901 A. Rodger & Co, Port Glasgow. **T** 1,206g, 729n.
D 230.2ft (70.16m) bp x 42ft (12.8m) x 11.5ft (3.35m).
E Tw scr, tpl, exp, 3 cyls, 130 NHP, 9 kts. By Ross & Duncan, Glasgow.
H Steel. 1 dk, flush; engines aft.
1901 Built for River Plate Fresh Meat Co as *Reformer*.
1914 Sold to Las Palmas Produce Co, owners of *Britanica* (27).
1923 Transferred to Union Cold Storage ownership.
1923 Became *Anglo No. 2*, owned by Union Cold Storage with Soc Anon Frigorifico as managers.
1935 Chartered to Cranston, Woodhead & Co; renamed *General Flores*.
1936 Reverted to *Anglo No. 2* and Frigorifico ownership.
1942 Became *Americano*.
1952 Sold to Sociedad Anonima Import y Export de la Patagonia; same name. Passed in the same year to Pedro G. Yachelini & Cia.
1957 Owned by Polar S.R.L.
1966 Broken up.